Introduction

747-400 rarity value and a great Qantas moment taken from the flight deck from London to Sydney on the QF002 operated by the -400 with Rolls-Royce engines. (Author)

INTRODUCTION
747: FOREVER QUEEN OF THE SKIES

To say that the Boeing 747 changed the world is more than an understatement. No other civil aircraft – not even Concorde – has had the global effect of the 747. For the 747 really has altered the world by having flown over 5.9 billion people – well over half the world's population. 747 really did touch lives, yet, incredibly, due to the rise of the twin-engined, long-range airliner and the critical effects of the Covid-19 pandemic and ensuing financial problems, we see the decline of the 747 (specifically as the 747-400) in passenger service; the final days of this airframe in mainline operations have occurred but, of course, recently built 747-800s will thankfully grace our skies for some time to come. Lufthansa might operate a few -400 passenger liners into an uncertain future, as might a few smaller operators.

This book takes off just as the mainline 747 fleet is prematurely grounded. So here is an opportunity to celebrate the life and times of what some say is the greatest airliner ever built: 747 – forever cited as the 'Queen of the Skies'. That overused phrase, icon, seems relevant. This book is designed to provide an accessible and value-for-money profile and tribute to this mighty aeroplane – or airplane.

First flown in 1969, with the one or two 747-300s still airborne, the last of the 747-400s enduring, and the new 747-800s likely to carry on for decades, the truth is that 747 in its classic variations served for 50 years. The electronic -400 still flies and may well do for years with cargo operators; the re-engineered -800 is fresh out of the box, so we could be looking at a total 747 service life of 75 years plus.

Rolls-Royce has bought the last example of the Qantas 747-400ER fleet to repurpose as an in-flight engine test airframe. Cargo-based 747 operations will continue for many years and in so doing will reverse the previous 747 hierarchy when passenger 747s topped cargo 747s for importance and style. We should note that America's Flying Tigers was the first scheduled cargo airline and has operated various 747s in that role.

What a shame it is that the 747-800 will not enjoy a sales renaissance. It is after all, the ultimate 747 and one so superb; the -800 is an airframe that recent world events have impacted upon, and if the A380 overextended its targets, the -800 exceeded its own as a final incarnation of 747 brilliance.

If the 747 was the ultimate twin-aisle, double-decker, widebodied airframe, the question is obvious – why build the Airbus A380? Apparently, the answer lay in prestige, politics and claims of technology, of new versus old. We are forced to observe that the A380 was not developed, not stretched and not enhanced. It served its expensive purpose and then it was terminated. So, the 747 'won' the battle, did it not?

Pure nostalgia of a great livery as the BOAC retrospective for 'BA 100' as the BOAC-liveried -400 is escorted by the Red Arrows; a rare view indeed. (Author)

Aviation enthusiasts all have their favourites – 707, DC-8, VC10, CV990, Comet, Caravelle, Concorde, Tristar, DC-10, 727 and A380, yet the 747 (from -100, -200 and the -SP, through to -300, -400 and to -800) arguably exceeds all airframes in its flying qualities, passenger experience and range-to-payload brilliance.

747 changed the airliner market and paradoxically created the twin-aisle, widebodied 'big-twin' concept – the 747 with two not four engines. Without 747, the mighty 777 would not have been what it is. Yet the ultimate development of the 747 – the -800 – will ply the airways for many years to come, in limited numbers with a few airlines.

During the heyday of the 747 in the late 1980s, it was reckoned that nearly 500 of them might be in the air at any one time around the globe – each carrying 350–450 passengers dependent on configurations and according to seat-plan and airframe type, including SP, SUD, EUD and Combi.

Joseph F. Sutter, the 747's chief project engineer, is a legend and so too is his aircraft. Jack Waddell was the man who flew the 747 into the air on its first flight. Thousands of other people created the 747. We do not have the space to name them all.

Whatever Boeing's recent self-inflicted wounds, we should never forget the stunning achievement that was, and remains, the 747 family. As a feat of engineering, as a piece of industrial design, the 747 is not just a hallmark, it is a moment in history. Sir Norman Foster, the architect, has correctly described the 747 in terms of architectural and structural genius.

Some people may criticize the concept of American exceptionalism and its flaws, but the Boeing 747 truly does frame an achievement of such order. Boeing has delivered 1,549 of its 747s and there are a few more -800s to come. As Boeing has pointed out, the 747 and the Apollo programme ran side by side and heralded two new dawns of aerospace: a truth not a boast.

In 747 and its development story, we can find one of the greatest engineering and industrial design stories in the history of mankind. 747 was safe, reliable and could recover itself from flight mishaps and engineering issues. Pilots loved this aircraft for all its features and its character. True, a few 747s have been sadly lost in service, but here was an aircraft that had it all. The addition of the Rolls-Royce RB211 engines – notably the later 500-series variants, the later revised General Electric and Pratt & Whitney powerplants – added even more ability to the 747. British Airways, KLM, Qantas, Cathay Pacific, Japan Airlines, Lufthansa, South African Airways and others are the core carriers who developed the ultra-long-range 747 routes and flights of 14 hours plus. Qantas created their unique 747-400 ER series. Korean Air's championing of the -800 should not go uncited in the hall of 747 fame. Pan Am's 747s ranged the globe, but on earlier engines and with more frequent stops.

As the big-twin (two-engined) airliners now dominate long-haul and over-ocean operations and, as the story of the four-engined Airbus A380 shows, the world is a different place thanks to the great gamble that Boeing took with its 747. From earlier, difficult days designing and proving the world's biggest-ever airliner, 747 has grown into a 400-ton leviathan capable of encircling the globe. Boeing took a massive multibillion-dollar gamble and won.

Above all, 747 is an aircraft with significant performance and one that had a global effect; it changed people's lives by opening up air travel to a wider market. The 747 helped forge today's airlines and their routes.

The oldest and greatest airlines have all been 747 operators. Launched with a first flight in February 1969 just as the 1960s closed, and into service with Pan American Airways across the Atlantic in January

Death of the Queen: BA -400 and ex-United Airlines -400 airframes of the wonderfully liveried Corsair fleet await their fate after final service in later 2020. All three aircraft had surpassed 100,000 flying hours each. (Author)

1970, 747 became the must-have four-engined, long-haul airframe.

With a range developed to 8,000 miles/13,000 kilometres, 747 can carry over 400 passengers in several classes. Japan Airlines once operated over 100 747s in the world's biggest 747 fleet, vying with British Airways for that title.

747 is held in affection by millions of people but perhaps none more so than the few hundred on board Captain Eric Moody's British Airways (BA) 747-200 G-BDXH on 24 June 1982. Flight BA 009, on its Kuala Lumpur–Perth sector of a UK–New Zealand trip, lost all four of its Rolls-Royce engines at night in an unseen cloud of volcanic ash. G-BDXH became a powerless 400-ton glider with a glide ratio of about 15:1 and soon began its fall of over 20,000 feet. After 13 minutes without thrust, a potential ditching was on the cards. Only superb training, brilliant 'team BA' airmanship and a fantastic aircraft with its systems and their integrity, saved the day. One engine was restarted as the aircraft descended towards 10,000 feet – just as the ditching was looking more likely – and then the other engines relit at reduced thrust, A relit engine then failed again. Moody landed the wallowing aircraft on three engines, 'blind' at night with an obscured windscreen and with several key systems out.

A nearly new KLM 747-400 Combi, PH-BFC on flight KL 867, suffered a similar fate over Alaska on 15 December 1989 and went on to a safe landing, but suffered over $70 million dollars' worth of damage. The aircraft glided down to 14,000 feet prior to an engine restart. On the way down, even the standby instruments were lost. Again, great training, great flying and a superb airframe saved the day. Real, hand flying, not computer-game skills, saved this 747 and its passengers – KLM being one of the world's leading trainers of pilots and a top safety-focused airline.

In these days of ultra-long-haul flights by 787 Dreamliners and A350s, some forget that it was a Qantas 747-400 that flew non-stop from London to Sydney as far back as 16 August 1989 when VH-OJA did the trip in 20 hours 9 minutes with a non-commercial load. Qantas also got 674 passengers (without luggage) into a 747 during an emergency rescue flight from Darwin in the 1974 cyclone disaster. There are further claims of nearly 1,000 people being crammed into a 747 on an emergency airlift flight.

The shorter-bodied -SP-specification 747s also ranged far and wide with several operators – the -SP being longer ranged and higher flying and perhaps a highlight for Pan Am's all-American 747 niche.

American enthusiasts will not forget the heady days of Pan Am, Braniff, Delta, Northwest, TWA and United 747s in all their guises. Throw in the oft-forgotten American Airlines 747s, Air Canada's 747s, CP-Air's orange beasties, Wardair's niche fleet, and you have a wonderful series of 747 legends.

As recently as 2020, the 747 set a new record with the fastest subsonic Atlantic crossing by an in-service airliner in a time of 4 hours 56 minutes, reaching a speed of 800mph/1,2987km/h – aided by the jet stream and storm winds. This beat the previous record of 5 hours and 1 minute held by a BOAC/BA VC10.

These are just a few examples of the 747's life cycle as the true 'Queen of the Skies' – as 747 enthusiasts call the machine. From the earlier analogue flight deck with dials and three or four crew including a flight engineer, to the -400's two-pilot, 'glass' cockpit with 'magenta-line' pilot flying and electronic operations devoid of a flight engineer, from a spiral staircase leading to a lounge, to an extended upper deck rammed with seats, 747 has evolved and now we have the ultimate 747, the -800.

747 is a stunning machine as well as a piece of social science and world history alongside its engineering achievement. It touched the world. As Qantas -400 fleet Captain Owen Weaver said, 'The 747 has a special place in the hearts of many Australians.'

The 100-year-old airline Qantas suddenly retired its historic 747 operations in 2020, the year of Covid-19, and British Airways did likewise alongside other operators. Thus was the 747 passenger-carrying story prematurely curtailed. The 747 era is passing. As of 2021, 747-800 remains in front-line service with Lufthansa, Korean Air, Air China, and the 747-400s might still fly with Lufthansa and other airlines such as Rossiya, China Airlines and smaller operators as well as cargo operators: Cargolux, CP Cargo, Air Bridge Cargo, Atlas Cargo, UPS, Polar Air Cargo, Silk Way, Qatar Cargo, Cargo Logic, which all still champion the 747.

The 'av geek' Sam Chui continues to pursue 747 nirvanas as the man who chases 747s – right to the end in the Mojave Desert 747 storage compound. From the Australian outback, across the African savannah, in European skies and the vast plains of North America, across great oceans, over all continents, 747 *has* touched lives. The creation of this aircraft, what went in to it and what the world's airlines did with it, is the core of the 747's story and of modern travel.

Enthusiasts, pilots, passengers and modellers all love the 747. Aircraft makers are now called 'airframers', but above all, one set of magical numbers define man's mastery of airline transport in the jet age. That set of numbers defines more than a brand, more than an aircraft: it frames a change upon the world. The number in question is of course the legendary badge – 'Seven Forty-Seven' or 747. Sadly, Boeing has just called time on even 747-800 production, a move forced by global economic conditions, not airframe related.

Herein, we embark upon a 747 tribute through full-scale and part-scale 747 reality. It's time to hit call 'V1' and then 'Rotate'.

The Aussies arrive. The Qantas -400 EUD big beast roars up to the stop point on the ramp at Sydney Airport. (Author)

Design by Dynamism

Pratt & Whitneys at polished perfection as the SAA 747 is towed to service on the ramp at London Heathrow prior to the overnight run to Cape Town. (Author)

'Vision' not accountancy lay behind the 747. Everyone knows that was the truth. This was a US$750-million project even at 1960s prices and currency rates, with an overall spend on the airframe and the construction facilities of over $5 billion at the prices of the day. We should not forget that the 747 launched a collection of tried and untried technological advances in a totally new concept. Bravery was required, as was money, patience and tenacity.

Often forgotten is the fact that in 1965 Boeing was focusing on a supersonic transport airliner – its ill-fated Mach 2.7-capable, 200+ seater '2707 SST' dream. At first Boeing's management saw the 747 as a project below the SST's status, but 747 soon became the prime focus, and the main risk, as SST faded in economic reality – its fiscal margin of error-to-success was less than a 10 percent fuel–cost variation.

As Boeing's Mr Sutter often stated of 747: 'Many people both inside and outside of Boeing, believed the programme life of a high-capacity subsonic jet would be short-lived because most long-haul traffic would be captured by the SST, which was planned to commence operation in the mid-1970s'.

The 747's starting point was military aviation and US Government DoD/USAF Operational Requirement CX-4 and its consequent outcome as a Heavy Logistics System (HLS) contract. This framed a requirement to provide a very large cargo and transport aircraft with the new high-bypass-ratio jet engines. In 1963, Boeing was studying such a machine – with a large forward-opening fuselage cargo door, deep 'double-deck' body and, at one stage, even a high wing. This of course was the same approach taken by Lockheed with its C5 Galaxy – the airframe that won the contract for such a heavy-lifter. But Boeing's work was not in vain, for it had outlined a theme – an airframe of 150 percent over the size of a 707. (Of interest, the later rival, the Airbus A380, was not to be the first very large, full-length, twin-deck airframe.)

Double-deck Legacy

Britain's Armstrong Whitworth had built a full-cabin, double-deck Ensign airliner in the 1930s in small numbers; near the close of the 1940's post-war environment the Bristol Brabazon had proved that a massive land-based airliner so configured could fly. The Saunders Roe Princess flying boat was also double-decked but didn't sell.

Boeing, with the Short Company, had built double-deck flying boats prior to 1939, and Dornier had put the flight crew in an upper-deck bubble on its Do X flying boat, but the true, full-length double-decker airliner was a product of the late 1940s and came from France. Such an aircraft was series-manufactured in France with piston engines and prop power by Breguet in its -761/-765 airframe, better known as the *Deux Ponts* airliner of 1949

The bird that started it all – the 707 prototype prior to being widened to become a true, big four-engined jetliner. (Boeing)

Building the first 747 at Everett as Boeing 'bet the farm' on its biggest gamble. (Boeing)

The original analogue flight deck had over 700 dials! (Boeing)

design and 1953 service introduction. This was the world's first viable, in-service, full-double-deck airline transport airframe and saw service with Air France and the French military.

Decades later, McDonnell Douglas proposed the MD-12 as a full-length, double-deck jet airframe, but it came along long after the ATL-98 Carvair Douglas DC-4 airliner conversion with its distinct upper deck lobe or bubble. In fact, both Douglas and Lockheed had created double-deck airline transport projects in the 1950s.

Boeing had of course built the -377 Stratocruiser with a small lower-deck cabin and lower cargo deck. A four-engine, jet-powered 367-64 version of this airframe was suggested as a double-decker airliner long before the 747 was born. A stretched 707-600 and a larger 800-series were also considered. Boeing even suggested a full-length, double-deck airliner in 1960, yet concerns over the sheer size of a double-decker and its operational, safety and evacuation problems precluded further development in the early 1960s.

Perhaps the most significant large double-deck airliner transport airframe prior to the 747 was the Lockheed R6V Constitution of 1946. Only two were built, but this was the largest, most aerodynamically sound, pressurized, double-deck airframe seen in the piston-power era. Pan Am was involved in it because of the very obvious long-range airliner potential.

The first proposals for a jet-age double-decker came from Boeing and Vickers in the form of the Super VC10 Superb.

1963–5 saw the outcome of the military studies CX-4 to CX-HLS and the procurement of the high-wing, high-bypass jet-engined C5 Galaxy military transport as the world's largest airframe to that date.

But Boeing, having lost this battle to supply the US military, repurposed its work on the project into the idea for an airliner. The prospect of a stretched 707 to compete with later DC-8 60-series of over 200-seat capacity enticed Boeing. But 707 with its short undercarriage legs and low-slung engines would not prove suitable for massive stretching. A clean-sheet design was required. Boeing's initial design studies for its new airliner *did* include a double-deck cabin (divided into structural zones fore and aft of the wing box) with doors on two levels; this design was smaller than the eventual 747 design. But the questions of safety, structure and evacuation remained unanswered. So, Boeing opted for the double deck only at the front of the fuselage and thus the front-loading cargo door option became inherent in the design.

Egged on by Pan Am's Juan Trippe, his stated ideas and his money, Boeing came up with a 20-foot-wide, 187-foot-long fuselage with a twin-aisle, nine- or ten-abreast main cabin seating plan and a new type of cargo container for underfloor storage, as well as the potential of nose-loading freight configurations. In fact, the airlines pushed Boeing to make the 747 even bigger than it had initially proposed.

The Sutter Effect

At 44, Joe Sutter was the dynamic lead on the 747 project. Less publicized but always credited by Sutter was the team led by the senior engineer on the design development of the 747, J. Beddinger, who pointed out that the 747's size would relieve congestion at already packed airports and in the air. Boeing engineer R. Brown advocated the widebody concept as senior Configuration Group engineer and could be said to be the leader of the design research psychology of the 747. E. Wells was a proven Boeing engineer who was vital to the 747's wing design and pylon-mounted jet engines. Contrary to some published opinion, Wells did not 'invent' or conceive the idea of a pylon mounted jet engine, but he did take the early research into such a configuration from wartime concept to on-the-wing reality for Boeing. W. T. Hamilton was Boeing's main wing-design man who complemented Joe Sutter's later lead. Hamilton solved many of the issues of the massive 747 wing and its origins in the B-52 wing experience. The lesser-known Malcolm Stamper was the head of Boeing's 747 project engineering programme.

Across the industry and Boeing's suppliers, 50,000 people worked on the 747 and its design and realization. At the Boeing factory 4,500 workers – specifically 2,700 design engineers – toiled night and day for several years. Pan American Airways' chief 747 development engineer, John Borger, was a key part of the aircraft's configuration development.

The 747s were built in the world's largest purpose-built factory, at Paine Field. Each 747 had six million parts, nearly 150 miles of wiring and weighed more than an express train. The developed 747 now weighs more than a commuter express train and has more parts.

Boeing famously 'bet the farm', risking its entire finances and existence on bringing the 747 to reality. It did so very quickly, but never at the expense of structure, safety or design. Boeing's then president, William Allen, took a major gamble with the 747 at a time when supersonic airliners and small, regional twin- or trijets were flavours of the day. Boeing's main preoccupation was surely with its brilliant 727 trijet that outperformed all its competitors.

The 747 was 231ft 10in/70.4m in overall length (fuselage 225ft 2in/68.63m) with a cabin length of 187ft/56.9m and width of 20ft 1in/6.1m; it was 64ft 3in/19.58m high to the top of the tailfin, with a wingspan of 195ft 8in/59.6m. The 747 -100 and -200, Classic were the vital widebodied heavy jet innovation: airlines would have no idea how to service the aircraft or its 400+ passengers. Everything was new and on a larger scale than any precursor airframe, including the Boeing 707 airliner.

Juan Trippe, the American airline transport legend, was the key to the 747's launch when his airline, Pan Am, ordered 25 747s in 1966, worth $525 million – all from seeing Boeing's plans and Sutter's models of the intended airliner. Without such a launch order, 747 would have stalled on the ground. Other American carriers soon signed up too.

Joe Sutter stated that the new 747 required 75,000 drawings, 4.5 million parts, 136 miles of wiring and 10 million hours of labour. But he was unaware that fitting externally supplied engines and making them work would become his biggest challenge.

Like many Americans, Sutter had European antecedents: his DNA came from an area of Bohemia in Central Europe that has produced some of the world's greatest engineers and designers in the field of aircraft, aerodynamics, cars and industrial technology and design. Names such as Porsche, Lippisch, Ledwinka, Jaray, Rumpler and many more stemmed from this enclave that existed prior to the remapping of Europe before the Second Wold War. Sutter – original paternal family name Suhadolc and maternal family name of Plesik – served in the US Navy in the Second World War and graduated as an engineer from university. So, we must put Sutter up there with the greats of design and note his place among the Bohemian DNA of engineering and design.

Sutter's original thoughts for the 747 were famously doodles on a napkin. He had learned much about wings and airliner handling as he developed the Boeing 367-80 into the 707 family and then directed design on the 727's superb parasol high-lift wing which had the largest leading-edge slats and multi-slotted trailing-edge flaps yet seen – which gave it a best-in-class takeoff and landing performance.

Sutter's own, personal design research psychology was what made the 747's safety standards so high – building in multiple fail-safe systems, redundant over-engineered features and cross-linked systems that could cooperate amid failure modes. But maybe that amazing 727 wing that led to the even more efficient 747 wing, really was the key.

Ex-Vickers BAC designers from the VC10 story worked at Boeing and assisted in the 'fail-safe' multi-system hydraulic and electrical systems as seen in the VC10 which had led with safety-first in design concept. Boeing's experience with the 727's vital T-tail and its hydraulically powered flight controls also transferred into the 747's hydraulic system design.

Sutter's fine autobiography (co-authored with Jay Spenser), *747: Creating the World's First Jumbo Jet and Other Adventures from a Life in Aviation*, fully detailed the trials and triumphs of achieving the incredible

Early 747s had nine seats across in economy class – and the seats were thickly padded with at least a 34-inch seat pitch. Such comfort was soon to be removed in a ten-across, lightweight seating configuration often with a 31-inch seat pitch. That is a fold-out cinema screen on the central bulkhead. (BA)

747 in great quality. Four flight control systems, four hydraulic systems, four main undercarriage units, four engines, and major structural load path safety features, all went in to the safety-first 747.

Designing and building the 747 was a huge challenge and involved new fields of aerospace technology. Problems developing the engines put the whole programme at risk. Yet the issues were solved and the 747 flew and handled like a dream – belying its size and sheer scale. In profile and in planform 747 was eerily similar to the shape of the Boeing F-86 Sabre jet fighter with its front end bubble canopy, swept wings and stylish tailfin.

The 747-100 was two and half times bigger than the mighty 707 Intercontinental series – the largest 707. The 747-400 and then the -800 were to be bigger still.

Two aisles, an upper deck, massive cargo holds and superb payload-range figures, were what made 747 pay – and achieve up to a 30 percent improvement in operating costs over older jet airliner types. 747's structure was strong but light, and like all airliners would require preventative structural work and corrosion inhibition. The fuselage hoops and stringers had classic Boeing anti-tear design to stop a crack or rupture spreading. The rear pressure bulkhead was rather large but strong. All apertures were reinforced, notably the heavily used doors and frames. A multi-panel rudder and rudder ratio mechanism ensured fail-safe control. The huge wing box and central torsion structure made the 747 really stiff where it mattered. A multi-spar wing carried the tension and compression loads and was strong, yet flexible enough to absorb stresses. The wings would 'bend' over ten feet before being at structural risk.

Safe Structure

The 747 used 147,000lb/66,150kg of ultra-high-grade, high-strength aluminium in its structure. The sheer strength of the 747 was shown when a China Airlines 747-SP (N-4522V), as Flight 006 on 19 February 1985, rolled into a

gross height excursion after stalling at very high altitude (41,000ft/12,500m) in the cruise after it lost speed following an engine failure. The crew suffered cognitive and spatial disorientation. Having rolled, spiralled and nose-dived 30,000ft/9,000m with over 5g recorded and then flown into a recovery at very high Mach number, the -SP did not break its back and went on to land safely. However, portions of all the wings were damaged, the fuselage rippled and hydraulic failures were noted. So high were the g-forces that one of the main landing gears was forcibly pushed out through its doors to a deployed position. Major sections of both horizontal stabilizers broke off and a portion of elevator came off entirely (resembling wartime B-17 damage!), but the 747 survived stresses that tested its maximum design loads to the limit. Of note, the main wings were found to be bent upwards by several inches. Perhaps this was the 747s closest call to a 'survivable' proof-of-design event. Somewhat incredibly, the airframe was rebuilt and served many more years with other operators until its maintenance records caused it to be grounded by the Federal Aviation Administration (FAA).

Wing Sweep

35 degrees was deemed the optimal wing sweep during post-war tests, but at highest sweep, 747 achieved 37.5 degrees. The massive wing area was 5,500ft² (510.9m²). The long, clean, engine pylon design of the 747 reduced interference drag over the wing as best as could be achieved with current knowledge. Gaps were left in slats and flaps to avoid pylon, nacelle and exhaust interferences.

Sutter had been aerodynamics lead on the 707 and 727 and he had pushed wing aerofoil, flap and slat performance to new heights. Boeing's wind tunnel and its work on the swept wings of the B-47, B-52 and 707 all contributed to their past lessons. The B-52 wing was of particular note in terms of structural lessons and avoiding flutter. German wing-design experts were also to be found at Boeing in the 1950s, as was the case in the British aircraft industry.

For 747, the wing was the key ingredient and what a wing it was. With Fowler-type derived flaps but triple-slotted, aided by curvaceous leading-edge slats with in-board Krueger flap, thrust dampers, efficient ailerons and some outboard wing twist 'washout' to cure a small problem, the wing excelled. Viewed spanwise it looks like a visual sweep-angle change occurs outboard of the outer engine, yet this is a function of the designed-in wing twist changes.

Design Details
747-100 & -200B Classic

Widebodied 300+-seat design with global sector range (4,000mi/7,980km of -100 to 5,820mi/10,780km of -200B) and excellent payload-range capabilities.

Four hydraulic systems for controls activation – no manual reversion required: seamless hydraulic piping, split systems, dual activation; mechanical linkages cannot be jammed.

Variable incidence stabilizer.

Artificial 'feel' units to three main flight controls.

Multi-channel electronic autopilot.

Innovative 18-wheel undercarriage with 16-wheel main gear of multiple bogies and axles.

Highly swept, advanced aerofoil section, lightweight, high-strength 'wet' wing with integral fuel tanks.

Multi-spar wing construction with composite construction wingtips. Integral engine pylon mountings.

Triple-slotted flaps (not on -SP) and highly effective leading-edge devices of 13 deployable sections of pneumatically actuated slats and in-board Krueger sections.

Upper deck lobe with passenger seating (latterly extended).

Underfloor cargo compartments with roller floor mechanism for new container and pallet designs.

Four high-bypass turbofans.

Twin aisle cabin with up to 10-across seating in standard classes.

Underfloor galleys and lifts.

747-100 fuel capacity: 48,445US gal/183,380l.

Max takeoff weight of -100 with JT9D engines: 710,000lb/322,49kg.

Max takeoff weight of -200B with RR D4 engines: 833,000lb/377,840kg.

Roll-out

Rolled out on 30 September 1968, but unable to fly until 9 February 1969 due to the engines problem, 747 was delayed and the crippling costs mounted. The original 747 was the Classic, recognizable because it had just three upper-deck windows on each side of its lobe or hump. The basic 747 would become the -100 series, as the revised B variant of December 1968 went on to become the -200 variant. A conversion pack latterly allowed ten windows per side on the -100, and of course the -200 and -200B became the multi-window standard. Conversely, 10-window -200 production models could have blanks applied. The upper-deck escape door was on the port side (only) on these early machines. The 18-wheel undercarriage with four-truck main gear could be landed with one (or both) outer main wing gear truck retracted.

The Engine Issues

Pratt & Whitney created their first high-bypass-ratio jet turbine in the JT-9D engine for the Lockheed C-5 Galaxy project – which Boeing had lost out to for military orders. Lockheed gave General Electric a head start by choosing its new high-bypass engine, not Pratt & Whitney's. So, Pratt & Whitney repurposed the engine and its first application came along for the 747 as Boeing evolved the design programme into reality.

Use of titanium, nickel and high-quality alloys gave strength and durability in the engine. Unlike the Rolls-Royce RB211 500-series engine which was a three-spool/core engine (the first such type), the Pratt & Whitney engine was a shorter, two-core, high-pressure combustion design that was easily identifiable by its big fan compressor housing at its front and then the 'tube' or pipe-type rear section leading to the exhaust. With a single main inlet fan, then a three-stage low-pressure compressor of smaller dimensions, leading to multiple-chamber compressor and turbine configuration, the engine weighed in at 8,608lb/3,905kg. The thrust component came out at a healthy 43,500lbf/193kN, but it was to be sufficient rather than in excess. Later competitor engines went to over 50,000lbf/229kN of thrust. But the original JT9D-3A reached its -7J variant (used in the later 747-200s) at 48,650lbf/216.4kN in 1974, going on to a final rating of 56,000lbf/243.5kN by 1982, and as the JT9D-7RH4H1 by 1985.

The early specification JT93A really was marginal for long-haul, high-takeoff-weight 747 applications in difficult conditions

The flight engineer's panel on an analogue-driven 747, three sets of eyes being safer than just two. (Author)

such as high temperatures or higher runway elevations. Pratt & Whitney knew it had to deliver more thrust and a constant series of 1970s–1980s variants delivered that thrust by increment. The competing RB211-524 B/C/D/H/J-series engines offered between 49,120lbf/234.6kN and 59,450lbf/264.4kN pounds-per-foot thrust rating.

The JT9D engine (and the other types) was mounted onto the wing pylon points by a series of simple yet strong titanium bolts. The engine was deliberately designed to snap from such fuse-bolt mountings and break free above a certain level of failure loading in terms of rotational, g-force or impact. Sixty-seven of the original JT9D new engines were to be destroyed in the development and testing programme.

The engine's first thrust-producing flight was from a position hanging off the wing pylon of a Boeing B-52 in 1968. This would provide differing pylon load paths and airflow patterns which some suggest may have been relevant to the issues that became apparent on the 747 wing. Three years' work would result in late certification, in early 1969, but problems with the fan blades touching the engine casing as it flexed under applied thrust load proved hard to isolate and resolve. The round engine casing flexed to an ovaloid shape under such load, and deformation allowed fan blades to grind against metal. A special reinforcing frame had to be worked into the main casing structure with a thrust yoke Y-framed metal brace being created by Boeing and Pratt & Whitney.

At one stage Boeing was left with many newly finished 747s parked up at the Seattle factory with no engines available; the airframes required weights to be applied at the pylon mountings to balance the aircraft for static storage.

Early engines needed to have the thrust increased for takeoff by a very gentle throttle 'stand up' – the levers could not be 'slammed' forward, nor powered down too rapidly as this would impose stress on the engines as they spooled-up or -down and could lead to a flame-out. Variable inlet panels on the cowlings also featured on early designs for the engine, but were soon deleted. Crosswind or turbulent airflow stalling in the engine fan inlet mouth could also lead to overheating and again a solution had to be found.

Joe Sutter stuck with the JT9D but had to make the men from Pratt & Whitney realize that they were all in serious trouble and that the engine needed fixing. Graphic in-flight demonstrations of engine problems (such as an induced compressor stall) when Pratt & Whitney's engineers were on a test flight, soon rammed the message home.

There is little doubt that the early 1970s JT9D engines had issues and several uncontained engine failures occurred in airline service – they always do – but it is just the causation and frequency thereof that

became an early 747 issue. Weak points in rivets inside the turbine compressors leading to a failed disc and rupture were a soon-solved problem. The 747 had growing pains with its engines and some issues with its flaps and undercarriage that needed resolving, but 747 became a tough old bird and one to be relied upon. Like the 707, a hard-used 747 was to be maintenance intensive. Get that right and the 747 would go on for decades. But, like any mechanical device, weak maintenance could affect the 747's dispatch reliability, flight performance and value.

First Flight

First flight of 747-100 airframe No. 1, RA 001, was on 9 February 1969 from Boeing's Paine Field at Renton Plant. The 300-ton aircraft with 1,000lb of water ballast on board (in lieu of seats and passengers) and much heavy-test instrumentation left the ground at a moderate 162mph and climbed out with the gear initially left down, as on all first flights.

After a 1-hour-15-minute flight RA001 was brought back for the first-ever jet-type upper-deck landing. The test flight had been terminated in an act of caution due to a sound being heard when Flaps/30 had been deployed in-flight – suggesting a widely cited possible issue with the massive triple-slotted flaps as they ran down their

Top: The classic form of the early 747 slips down onto the runway threshold at 150 knots and flaps 30. (Author)

Above: Pratt powerplant needing attention: JT9D innards exposed during maintenance. (Author)

BA blue on early -100 Pratt engines at Heathrow in the Landor livery. A bit of a smoker there perhaps? (Author)

tracks; it turned out to be the first flap lead section becoming slightly misaligned. First flight crew; Jack F. Wadell (Commander), Bien Wygle (Co-pilot), Jess Wallick (Flight Engineer). Wadell was an ex-Navy pilot – as so many US airline pilots have been – so he knew how to put a big plane down very accurately 'on the numbers'.

1,400 hours on flight testing followed, notably including tail-strike takeoffs, go-arounds, wet runway testing and, of note, stall and spin testing. Landing the big machine from a flight deck 30 feet up in the air proved to be a new skill; pilots tested such height-related issues out on a special test rig created by Waddell. This allowed them to adjust their perceptions for the fact that the aircraft's wheels touched the ground long before their 'senses' would do so, perched up high in the bubble top as they were.

Waddell stated at the time that the 747 simply flew itself down the glidepath in total stability, flaps and speeds being coordinated in a classic 3-degree nose-up, power-on approach on finals at 160 knots. 'Pilots will love it,' said Waddell adding, 'It almost lands itself.'

The 707's high-speed landing requirements had been tamed: here was the 747 that offered stability, time and easy handling on the approach and it could be landed with maximum weight at less than 150 knots (280km/h) in the right configuration – the slower-speed landing/approach stability was a huge safety factor for pilots, especially in more difficult weather conditions. The only other large civil aircraft that offered such a low-speed, stable landing at the time was the BAC/Vickers VC10 and Super VC10. Due to its larger size and weight, 747 was not quite as slow as VC10 on finals over the runway threshold, but it certainly added safety by reducing landing speeds to the 140–150 knots touchdown speed zone. A commercial -200B could land at weight at 141 knots (261km/h) and even the -300 only added slightly to that speed. A 747-SP

(with load) could land as slowly as 137 knots (254km/h).

Despite its size, 747 responded directly to the controls without lag. It turned and banked with alacrity and showed none of the expected heaviness associated with a very large airframe. 747 also had a rudder ratio (deflection) device and adjustable tailplane incidence settings, both features that allowed the pilot to fine-tune the aircraft to its needs.

On 30 December 1969 the 747 received its official airworthiness certificate, but Pan Am had had to cancel its original launch date for 747's entry into service; Pan Am's first transatlantic proving flight also suffered engine problems. Pan Am's first scheduled 747 service on 22 January 1970 was delayed by overheating issues and a substitute airframe had been wisely placed on hand in reserve. The JT9 engine remained sensitive to tailwind airflow conditions at start-up.

Water-injection, Blow-in Intakes & ARS

Water injection to early JT9-3A engines was added to aid takeoff performance. Improved turbine-blade design and inner core low-pressure combustion chamber changes all helped the JT9D become more reliable and more powerful. Rolls-Royce would of course go through very difficult times with its unique RB211 fan-blade design and its inherent issues.

Prior to mid-1971, early 747s were built with -3A engine nacelles that had circumferential moveable panels around the front of the engine casing intake lip. These were doors that opened as blow-in doors which opened up on takeoff to feed extra airflow into the main front fan. From 747 line number 154, these doors were removed in favour of a larger-mouthed intake/casing (as also applied to -7-series JT9D engines). Of interest, many older engines fitted to earlier 747s were modified to remove these old blow-in door intake casings and therefore this design feature is often forgotten by younger 747 enthusiasts.

The JT9D latterly benefitted from an Automatic Recovery System (ARS) with extra bleed air valves designed to lessen compressor stall in forward thrust setting. A special thrust reverse bleed air system was applied to do the same thing during thrust reversal down to 55 knots prior to cancellation of the reversers. Fan-blade rivets were also to be improved to reduce flexing under load. Records show that very early JT9D high-pressure turbine core fan blades could reputedly become damaged beyond efficient use in under 500 hours.

The JT9D engine was to be developed into the PW 4000-series which would compete with the rival Rolls-Royce RB211 and General Electric CF6-50D (first GE-powered 747 flight on 26 June 1973) engines on the 747s wings. The US military 'proved' the early use of the GE engine on the 747 airframe.

Climb Performance Issues

Heavily laden to max-weight 833,000lbf/ 377,840kg, the early 747-100 might require 10,000ft/3,200m of runway to rotate and leave the ground. At very high operating temperatures and also with altitude effect, this might extend to 12,000ft/3,657m. As engine power ratings increased, shorter takeoff distances became more normal.

A very poor climb rate, counted off slowly by per-100ft increment (notably in high operating temperatures) did not just afflict the early -100s with the JT9D-3a engines in tropical region conditions because, even a hot summer's day at London Heathrow might see a fully fuelled Pan Am or TWA 747 heading direct to the US West Coast, almost stagger into the air near the far end of the 11,000ft runway and take a long time to get to 10,000ft altitude – perhaps over 30 minutes, somewhere over the Midlands or Wales depending on routing.

Eastbound departures from London Heathrow (runway 10R) for such westbound long-haul flights meant that any engine failure on climb-out was a very serious affair as the city of London lay directly beneath and a tight turn westward was not possible, as heavy, slow aircraft cannot be turned sharply without speed decay and risk. Screaming 747s in a very shallow climb heading up the Piccadilly railway line or the A4 highway was an oft-cited joke, but not a laughing matter for flight crews. Most of the passengers remained in blissful ignorance; on the flight deck, a certain degree of apprehension may have been apparent.

Growing Pains

A bigger, safer, slower to land, strong, reliable 747 was more than 707 development – it was a whole new world. Pilots and passengers adored it. Boeing had hit the bull's eye. The only real operational issue was that the airlines and the airport operators had no prior experience in dealing with such a leviathan and the number of passengers it could hold and disgorge.

Because of the earlier problems with engines and their late delivery, Boeing had a reserve of completed 747s ready-built but parked up, which explains why, once the engines were certificated and fitted, mass deliveries were quickly made in 1970/1 to the world's major airlines.

Meal services on early 747 flights were slow as crews learned to use all the galleys and systems. A 747 arrival at an airport might clog up the ground handling facilities; several 747s arriving at once would cause chaos. As 1970 rolled onward, airlines were forced to keep up and order 747s.

However, in the early 1970s, the lack of thrust and the temperament of the JT9D engines in early -3A guise became a continuing in-service issue. Ferrying a fifth engine in the special underwing engine pod that the 747 was designed with, soon became a regular sight across the Atlantic. In the worst-case scenario, an arriving 'five-engined' 747 bringing in a spare engine for another 747, might suffer an engine failure and require its own engine replacement.

747-100 or Dash 100 was to be the revised name for the upgraded launch model and a series of line improvements were incorporated into these airframes built in 1969/70. Boeing revised the 747 specification, adding revised parts and a definitive 747 B variant was framed in October 1970 that delivered the improvements. These included stronger structures in the main undercarriage and fuselage and more fuel tankage. This higher-weight 747 B was effectively the precursor of the -200 and -200 Super B branded airframes. Confusingly, Boeing then created the retrospective -100B. This belated, somewhat illogical airframe specification was kept as a production variant for some years longer than many realize, with nine -100Bs built towards the end of the 1970s and long after the -200B had begun its classic reign.

The improved -200 variant, as the defining -200B, was soon to be offered with engines from manufacturers other than

JAL birds rest at Tokyo Narita by night with a -300 fronting a -100. (Author)

Pratt & Whitney (General Electric from June 1973 on; Rolls-Royce from 1976). Confusingly, Pan Am had their early-build -100s upgraded to the B specification but called them -100A variants. By October 1972 Boeing had announced the short-range, high-capacity -100SR variant. Throw in the fact that very early 747s were cited with their Boeing customer number excluding the -100 nomenclature and the record gets even more confusing.

A 747F Freighter arrived in November 1971 with the massive upward-swinging nose and reinforced floor and cargo-handling systems. The 747C Convertible version of 1973 added the option of all-cargo or all-passenger configurations and the airline customer could also make the most of the new side cargo door (rear main deck) as the SCD option. These SCDs as original builds and later conversions further muddied the 747 references. Add in the first -100 converted to SCD status in February 1974 (Sabena's OO-SGA) and, then in March 1975, the first SCD-equipped -200M Combi (Air Canada's C-GAGA) as the

Old airframes need constant work. These reinforcing plates around a main cabin door are typical of the extra work needed on a hard-worked, high-time 747. (Author)

first production-line Combi, and clarifying the 747's production nomenclature and history gets even tougher.

747-100SR

This was a 'special' high-density, short-range 747 for frequent short-flight cycles with reinforcements to the undercarriage, reduced fuel capacity to reduce weight and loading fatigue on the structure. Dating from launch in 1973, the SR had an internally extended short-top upper-deck design to cram in more passengers, but the rare later variants of the SR, as BSRs, had early use of the extended upper deck seen on the -300. Early -100SRs had a 498-passenger capacity in two classes: later an extended upper deck (EUD) -100 BSR could accommodate up to 550 in one main class, with a small J-Class business section – 563 seats was the highest single-class configuration. Seven of the 100-SRs were built. Further -100 'specials' included 20 -100BSRs and two -100 BSREUDs, for Japan Airlines (JAL) and All Nippon Airways (ANA) respectively.

First service of the standard or short-top-100SR was in 1973 and was developed for sub-1,000-mile Japanese domestic high-cycle, high-density (with limited galley and in-flight service delivery) domestic-route operations, likely to put a lot of strain on the airframe due to repeated short flight and pressurization cycles. Boeing upped the design to 52,000 flight cycles. The engines were Pratt & Whitney JT9D-7A or -7F types. The -100BSR was the later development with an increase in maximum takeoff weight. The JT9D-7F or General Electric CF-6-45 were the favoured engines.

Pratt & Whitney later created the PW 4056 turbofans of much higher thrust, of over 55,000lbf/240kN rating. This engine, although efficient, had an appetite for Stage 5 combustion parts – which needed regular maintenance.

The key 747 model evolution became -100, -100SR, -100BSR/SUD, -100B and -100F/SCD. The shorter -SP was a unique 747 variant. Latterly there would come -200, -200B (SuperB), -200C, -200F and -200M (Combi). Following on was the short-lived -300, -300SR and, of note, the -300M (Combi).

This old beast shows off the Freighter configuration; you can just see the nose-lifting shut line. (Author)

Boeing 747-100 Technical Specification

World's first widebodied, twin-aisle, four-engined jet airliner.

Flight crew x 3; cabin crew x 18.

Passenger capacity: 366–452 with 480 maximum one class.

Wing span: 195ft 8in/59.64m.

Wing area: 5,500ft²/511.0m².

37.5-degree sweep.

Aspect ratio of 6.96.

Length: 231ft 4in/70.51m.

Height: 63ft 5in/19.33m.

Cabin width: 20ft/6.1m.

Underfloor freight: 6,190ft³/173.3m³.

Max T/O weight: 735,000lbf/333,400kg.

Max fuel capacity: 48,445USgal/183,380l.

Max payload: 76,800kg.

First flight: 1969.

Initial powerplant: Pratt & Whitney JT9D-3A, then -7-series.

Max speed: 523kts/602mph.

Mach: M.82 (cruise), MMo: Mach 92.

Engine-driven 60kVa generator to give 15/200V three-phase AC electrical systems with added DC systems and APU AC power supply.

Pan Am's venerable fleet really were hard worked and carried some fairly noticeable dents, scars and patches into their later service. *Clipper Black Sea* slides down the skyway. Note the three-window upper-deck status. (Author)

Pan American and Beyond

Pan Am, as its title and 747 livery would announce, written large all over the fleet, launched the 747 and made others follow. At one stage there were 66 747s in Pan Am's passenger 747 fleet, and several more freighter/cargo variants. The fleet total touched 77 airframes across the operating period.

As launch customer, it was Pan Am and its maintenance crews and ground engineers that did a huge amount of the early in-service work to prove the original 747 into reliable airline service and to get the 747 over its initial service-entry issues and dispatch delays – before the references became -100 and -200 series.

Pan Am's Clipper Constitution made the first (delayed) transatlantic commercial service 747 crossing to London in January 1970. Pan Am operated a non-stop New York–Moscow service early on, and operated a round-the-world global route using -100s, -200s and of course, the -SPs. Frankfurt became a major Pan Am hub from which India was just one Pan Am flight away.

Early Pan Am -100s had nine-across seating in Economy Class, not the ten-across that soon became a more cramped normality for most airlines, including Pan Am. Pan Am's so-called Business Class was in fact a standard row of Economy Class seats with the middle seat blocked off where possible, which often meant you paid a higher fare but received an Economy Class product. Following Qantas and KLM innovating proper larger Business Class seats, Pan Am responded with the widest Business Class seat on the market and called their offering Clipper Class.

When withdrawn from service, the Pan Am -100s were best described as well used. The need for extra rivets, reinforcing plates, drilled cracks, corrosion repairs and ongoing fail-safe maintenance were all part of the operating history in the Pan Am fleet. Pan Am's 747s also became part of the USA's State Reserve fleet of civilian aircraft which is where the side cargo door (SCD) option originated on -100 airframes.

Pan Am started the sell-off of its 747 Clipper Cargo fleet in the 1980s, but at one stage operated, not only its own -100F (-123F) freighters, but also a -200C (-273C) leased in from World Airways.

Eastern Airlines leased three 747s (-100s) from Pan Am in a rare and short-lived domestic 747 operation from 1971 to 1973, which was more of a marketing exercise than fleet procurement. Two of the airframes wore full Eastern livery. A further two (ex-Qantas) 747s were to be purchased for intended European routes but did not make it onto those routes. The Eastern 747 experiment soon lapsed.

TWA

Trans World Airlines' (TWA) -100 fleet (to total 27) entered service early with most being delivered in 1970/1. Ultimately, over 30 747s would operate in TWA colours, a small number in comparison to other major airlines. As late as 1995, TWA was adding -100s to its fleet and it would be a TWA -100 that closed the airline's 747 chapter near the end of 2000. Often less than visible today, were TWA's three -SPs, one of which was leased to American Airlines for some time. TWA's seven -200s were operated by TWA from 1986 to 1998.

At their height, the red-and-white-hued TWA 747s flew in fine style with excellent cabins, good leg-room and wide seats, notably in the premium classes – Ambassador Class was a TWA highlight.

In the late 1980s Pan Am deployed large, bold fonts for its titles. This 747 was seen at Paris CDG. (Author)

But as with the Pan Am machines, they were hard-worked, ageing and lower powered. Quite a lot of fatigue repairs and heavy maintenance were to prove relevant. The -100 that crashed as Flight TWA 800 had in fact flown an astounding 100,000 hours plus with over 18,000 landings on the logbook. In fact, TWA operated five -100 veterans with between 90,000 and over 100,000 hours per airframe. Cracks, corrosion, skin repairs and major rebuild work had all been required to keep these ageing airframes safe. Yet, when you got on board a TWA 747, you touched the soul of American aviation: the flight and cabin crews were proud and the airline an icon. Sadly, it is long gone.

The crash of Flight 800 near New York on 17 July 1986 was a sad moment in TWA's 747 history – a well-used -100 of 24 years' service.

United Airlines

Veteran carrier United Airlines (UAL) operated its 747s in several iconic colour schemes, perhaps none more so than the original Friendship tagged white and be-striped livery of the 1970s. United became America's second major 747 operator and flew its first on 26 June 1970 – as did Continental Airlines. United had 44 examples in use at its highest 747-ownership period and would also lease in others. United absorbed part of the ex-Pan Am -SP fleet, while United's later -400s went on to another life with other carriers – notably at Corsair.

The United or UA/UAL-coded 747s ranged far and wide, notably in the Pacific and Asian arenas including a Proud Bird of the Pacific -100. United had one -100 that had over 90,000 hours on the airframe – not bad for an early bird.

Perhaps less well known in Europe than Pan Am or TWA, United had huge profile in the USA and the Pacific Rim arena, taking over Pan Am's transpacific routes, and reached across to Hong Kong, Tokyo, Guam, Singapore, Sydney and beyond – including Vietnam, China and New Zealand. Flight UA800 became a favourite for America-bound transpacific passengers. United's 747s (including three -SPs) created a massive brand and a loyal following among passengers, 'av geeks' and airline crews alike. Despite the age of some of its fleet, the brand remained a high-quality and popular offering. The superb flying skills of a United crew (under Captain Cronin) saved a 747 and its occupants on 24 February 1988 when the United -100's front cargo door mechanism failed and ripped a large hole in the airframe, resulting in explosive decompression and engine and handling issues at night over the Pacific Ocean. Several passengers were sadly ejected, but the aircraft made a safe emergency landing at Honolulu.

United retired its last 747, a -400, in 2018, and in so doing became the longest-running American 747 operator.

Northwest Orient (NWO)/Northwest Airlines (NWA)

Previously known as Northwest Orient (NWO) – a title that referenced its northwestern and transpacific activities – the airline was latterly rebranded as

Northwest (Orient) made the most of its red-hued livery as seen on this big American airframe awaiting service. That flight deck is a long way up. (Author)

Northwest Airlines (NWA) but retained its red tail and red primary colour element.

Founded in 1926 and deceased in 2010 via a merger with Delta, NWO was a major 747 customer. NWO operated a large fleet of dedicated 200F cargo lifters (up to 15) on an extensive freighter network in the 1970s and 1980s. The airline's first passenger-configured -100 was delivered in October 1970 and registered as N601US. After 11 more -100s were purchased, NWO took 25 -200s. NWO took the development -400 airframe N401PW which then became N661US (later in Delta Airlines service).

In their always-distinct liveries across four decades, the fleet made a huge mark on American airline transport history and Pacific passenger and freight operations and were fondly regarded by many crews and passengers alike for a distinct brand identity and service. It was Northwest that suffered the rudder 'hard-over' mechanical incident on a -100, on 9 October 2002, en route to Japan. No accident resulted due to superb airmanship and asymmetric thrust skills, but this was a major late event in the 747s history and led to airframe/airworthiness (not operator) outcomes. The flight crew were recognized for their feat of recovery from major control issues and un-commanded extreme bank angle excursion.

American Airlines: a Silver 747 Fleet
Often forgotten was the fact that American Airlines (prior to its DC-10 and MD-11 obsession) was a 747 operator. At its recent height, AA operated a mind-boggling 875 aircraft, but even back in the late 1970s, its fleet numbered in the hundreds. Curiously, from being a key Boeing 707 and 727 player, it was less taken with the 747 and operated a relatively small fleet. But that did not stop it creating a unique cabin configuration with a rear, cabin and main deck lounge area as well as sporting an electric self-playing piano. The AA -100s (as -123s) had the rare lower-deck galley configuration.

In 1970, AA secured delivery options for 15 -100s, the first airframe delivered being manufacturer line number 46. AA also leased in an ex-Pan Am machine in which the blue Pan Am cabin décor was quickly obscured by the addition of some AA red-hued seat headrest covers. Seven -100s were quickly delivered but with nine more to follow. But many of the fleet were to be converted to 'American Freighter'-liveried cargo configuration: it was 1984 before AA took a single -200C. Two years later the impressive sight of two AA -SPs in polished metal finish added lustre to the 747's history. Seeing both N601AA and N602AA parked next to each other at Flughafen Frankfurt Main really drove home the power of the 747 story. However, the pair was mostly seen on the Dallas–Tokyo service – ultra-long range -SP territory for sure.

Of note, American leased in a TWA -SP which eventually ended up as a religious ministry aircraft delivering missionary and humanitarian efforts. American had also used its -SP airframes on the Dallas–Honolulu routing in the early 1980s. The AA -200C was in service for less than 18 months, but the -SPs served under a decade in silver-winged colours. The ex-AA -100 N9963 performed United's last -100 passenger flight in 1999.

AA swapped its 747 fleet out with Pan Am in exchange for ex-domestic National Airlines/Pan Am DC-10s, with which it had become very much taken. Braniff used one ex-AA 747. An ex-AA -100 airframe eventually went to a life at Highland Express and at Virgin Atlantic Airways. One AA 747 was converted to transport the Space Shuttle as a 747-SCA (another SCA was ex-JAL). Another went to TWA and thence to a VIP role with the UAE Government. AA's 747 freighter fleet had second lives with the likes of Trans Mediterranean, Flying Tigers and UPS. AA did not move to the -300 or the -400 as it preferred the operating economics of the trijet and had no major long-range 747 requirement.

Continental Airlines
Continental's first 747 arrived in May 1970 but it would latterly acquire earlier-built -100s and -200s with the earliest being Boeing line number 36. Continental initially operated six -100s and then from the mid-1980s, seven, then ten -200s which in several cases came to the airline from Qantas, Lufthansa and Alitalia. Continental had ordered four new-build -100s from Boeing, mostly for service use on Pacific routes, with comfort to the fore, and in certain configurations, just 299 seats – a very low seat-per-mile cost-base index for a 747 operator. Latterly resplendent in the (expensive to apply and fly) full-coverage golden colour scheme, the Continental name was also applied to the Continental Micronesia operation, mainly served by a suitably titled -200B that originated as Alitalia's I-DEMB, then to serve Continental's main fleet prior to serving in Micronesia from 1995 to 2002, notably on the Guam–Tokyo and Hawaii services.

Continental 747s also served European routes such as New York (EWR) to Paris, Madrid and London Gatwick, as well as forays to Frankfurt. Auckland and Sydney were also occasionally served by Continental's rather vintage 747s.

A more modern livery (white/blue) replaced the famous gold tail. The airline's last 747 service came in 1997, operating the Honolulu/Guam–Tokyo Narita shuttle (an overnight return flight) prior to the airline using trijets. Certain Continental 747 Tokyo flights originated at Seattle (SEA) and then from Houston, Texas (IAH). Despite being famed for its history, individuality and character, Continental was absorbed into the corporate amalgamations of the major US airlines around the 1990 crisis and via its People Express (PE) connection and operated hybrid-livery PE/CO 747s. With Texan shareholdings and, from 2010 further corporate moves, Continental was then to disappear under United's colours.

Delta Airlines

Atlanta-based Delta Airlines gave its 747s a noteworthy livery design and it is significant that the last American operation of a 747 passenger-type airframe by a major airline was on 3 January 2019 when a Delta 747-400, as the last of the 16-strong Delta fleet, flew off to retirement. Delta's first 747 was a -100, line build number 101, delivered near the end of 1970. Delta flew five -100s, and used them very effectively on American domestic, transcontinental long-range routes and some forays overseas (including to London) up to 1977. Delta's -100 had an unusual upper-deck layout with the space divided into a lounge and a private suite – decades before a suite became a First Class or Business Class marketing tool.

Delta's DC-8s had flown to Europe so the 747s did likewise and excelled on US premium routes, but as early as 1974, Delta began to sell off its lovely 747s – they were labelled as too big for their transcontinental tasks. Trijets then ruled until, in 2009, Delta absorbed 16 ex-Northwest Airlines -400s when the carriers merged. Delta upgraded its -400s to a new Business Class specification between 2010 and 2012. Two -200 all-passenger 747s were part of the deal, as were the -200C freighters of Northwest. Here began a new, second Delta 747 chapter. Delta had not traditionally been a Boeing customer, but its original 747 operations were a vital part of its growth and operations. Delta also had nearly 90 Boeing 727s in its fleet. The -200s were soon sold off. One of Delta's 747 captains, Captain J. McMahan, was licensed to fly the 747, the DC-10 and the L1011 Tristar. Only three US pilots are known to have achieved such status.

Evergreen International would operate an early Delta -100 and it can now be found in the Evergreen Aviation Museum. Another ex-Delta -100 worked for Evergreen and then became the famous 747 water bomber firefighting 747.

Braniff operated a strangely liveried collection of 747s, notably the Big Orange, also known as The Great Pumpkin. Initially, the Braniff fleet was limited to one 747 and saw other 747 options cancelled. Then, ultimately, Braniff leased in 747s and served Europe and the Pacific Rim with its orange Ultra-liveried 747s. Originally, Braniff used the lone, new early-build -100 (the 100th built), but it was not until the early 1980s that a core -100 fleet of four -100s was established. Some of these were hybrid-livery ex-AA lease airframes, with orange stripes added as a Braniff identifier livery. Then came four -200 airframes, and, of interest, the three Braniff -SPs, with one, N603BN, flying for just over a year before going to Boeing. N604BN lasted eight months before going to Aerolineas Argentinas, and N6060BN served three years prior to sale to Pan Am. At its height, the Braniff 747 fleet

Above: One of Cathay's Freighters trundles along at Sydney with the cityscape framing the moment. Rolls-Royce power – of course. (Author)

Right: The rarer sight of a Kuwait Airways -200 as she is pushed back from the gate at Amsterdam Schiphol's D-Pier on a stormy day. (Author)

Lufthansa's classic -200B with GE power and the revised 1990s livery minus cheatline. (Photo Lufthansa)

totalled 11 airframes of varying provenance, ownership and leasing status. Braniff specified expensive cabin furnishings and colour trims including leather seats and sub-divided cabins.

National Airlines of Florida ordered two -100s which operated from late 1970 to 1975 on domestic routes with occasional foreign forays.

Tower Airlines/Tower Air (1983-2000) was a well-known second-tier 747 operator with 30 airframes in its all-747 fleet, many taken from TWA and Pan Am. New York-based it ran 15 of the -100 and 15 of the -200.

World Airways was a smaller American charter operator based in Atlanta and in 1973 it operated the first new-build -200C Convertible which included a nose door and the reversal of the cabin window deletes -- keeping the windows; meaning the airline could switch between freight and passenger configurations, notably for its U.S. military charters. World Airways took three such airframes and followed up with several -200s and finally a -400BDDF with which it ended its operating days.

Air Canada and Canadian Pacific/CP Air. These two Canadian airlines created a Canadian legend with their own particular brand of 747 operations: **Air Canada** (AC) ceased its 747 operations in October 2004 after 33 years of flying the 747. AC's first -100 arrived in 1971 and four more followed. The -200M fleet totalled three airframes. Latterly four -400 airframes arrived via the Canadian Airlines merger in 1990. Three -400Ms were also on the fleet. The original Air Canada livery saw a black-painted area on the nose of its 747s. This was unusual and its prime effect was to reduce glare into the windscreens, yet it was ultimately removed.

From late-1973 (delivery) through to 1986, **CP Air** operated four -200Bs (all delivered by late 1974) on routes to Asia, Australia, America and Europe. Eventually the fleet went into second-life service with Pakistan International Airlines. CP Air kitted its early 747s out internally with railwayana in an upper-deck bar in tribute to the company's railway origins. CP's livery

with its blend of red and orange paint with a polished metal nose and forward fuselage was unusual. CP Air's 747s were named as Empresses (e.g., *Empress of Suva*) as were the airline's other widebodies. The CP 747s were much loved by Canadians, as was the airline itself.

Canadian Airlines (International) emerged after CP Air was subject to merger in 1987 and the new Canadian Airlines became a newly branded and newly liveried airline that also absorbed the independent Wardair and gained its transatlantic routes. Canadian Airlines was absorbed by Air Canada in 2001.

Wardair, and Nation Air of Canada, both ran small fleets of much-loved 747s. High-quality Wardair operated five very comfortable, shiny 747s from 1973, before two -100s, and then two brand-new -200s with GE engines joined the fleet. Wardair's first -100 was a converted new undelivered airframe from a cancelled Braniff order and was cited as a -1D1 variant. Small but perfectly formed was the verdict of the airline by many of Wardair's 747 passengers and the airline is sadly missed.

Nation Air reputedly operated leased aircraft from 747-provider Air Atlanta Icelandic, but then operated its own 747 fleet. Nation Air variously employed six -100s and four -200s. Nation Air ceased trading in controversial circumstances after one of its DC-8s crashed.

747 Early Incidents and Survivability
Carrying more passengers than any other airliner, it was obvious that any accident would have larger implications. Boeing gave the 747 and its occupants the best chance of survival in a 'survivable' impact which good design engenders. This was

---

Other Notable American 747 Operators

Air National	United Parcel Service
Seaboard World Airlines	TransAmerica
Flying Tigers	DHL
Metro International	Federal Express
People Express	UPS
Kalitta Air	

'passive' (crash) safety, but 'active' safety in terms of handling, behaviour and operation is what set the 747 apart from the start. Pilots loved 747 for its superb handling and flying qualities, its reserves of safety in extreme attitudes and its 'safe' behaviour, notably on final approach in bad weather. However, every airliner, like every car, has its accidents and the 747 was not immune.

After 1970 service entry, all was quiet on the incident front until the first big 747 in-service incident occurred when the early Pan Am -100 flagship N747PA hit runway lights on takeoff from San Francisco on 30 July 1971 and sustained serious structural damage as it rotated and climbed out. Amazingly, the heavily impacted rear stabilizer and its spar retained structural integrity, as did the fuselage that had been penetrated – with the flight and systems controls affected. The aircraft returned and inevitably landed heavily but no one was killed. The 747 structure had saved a very serious day. After repairs this 747 flew with numerous African and second-tier operators but did in fact return to Pan Am service in the interim part of its life.

Three years later the first fatal 747 crash occurred, on 20 November 1974, when Lufthansa's early -100 D-ABYB *Hessen* crashed on takeoff from Nairobi. Due to an alleged combination of system designs, flight-deck procedures and crew training mechanisms, the 747 left the ground with an incorrect slat/Kreuger flap setting, leading to a stall just after rotation to climb angle. Fifty-nine of the 157 people on board died. As a result, Boeing made changes to the slat/flap takeoff configuration system and related warnings, and changes were also made to airline training processes. At least two previous events of the slat/flap systems engineering nature had been reported and potentially more unreported. It may have been that the necessary warning systems and alert lights were not functional on the *Hessen*, or perhaps inadequate.

The 747's takeoff configuration warning system did not allow or warn for a potential mishap where the relevant pneumatic valve was not open – as it should have been opened by a flight engineer. Design changes were made, and therefore citing 'pilot or crew error' seems to be a singularly unfair pronouncement within the overall systems-related functions. The circumstances and factors of this dysfunction were an unexpected and unrealized design issue that Boeing quickly attended to.

The -100 N7470 is the prototype of the original (-121) and is now on display at the Museum of Flight, Seattle. It was latterly reconfigured after its original test flying period. N747PA, the *Clipper Juan T Trippe* -121 airframe, ended up on display in South Korea but has been modified as a static exhibit.

KLM moment. Captured on the ramp at Schiphol, this early -200 with Pratt & Whitney power is making ready for the off to serve the Jakarta service in the final days of KLM's -200 operations. Isn't she lovely? (Author)

Developing the Queen of the Skies

From -100 Classic to -800 Upgrade

The next 1970's variation of the 747 was the -200 and it evolved across the following key configuration variations:

-200B from 1970
-200C (Convertible) from 1973
-200E4B from 1973
-200M (Combi) from 1974
-200F/SF (Freighter) from 1971 & 1974
-SP from 1975
-200B SUD/Conversion kit announced 1980
VC-25A/-2G4B from 1987
200B SCD (Side Cargo Door): note that SCD was not originally an official Boeing designation
SCD/C-19A Civil Air Reserve (CRAF) was a modified airframe definition as applied to Side Cargo Door conversions in US fleets; from 1985.
77-43 Corporate airframe (as HZ-HM1A)

Configured in late 1969 before the 747 achieved mainline operations, an improved baseline variant was soon launched into the sales arena. This improved 747 effectively became the B-model – to become the -200 – and the earlier-built machines retrospectively became commercially defined as the -100. Then the B-model confusingly became the -200B (tagged by some as the Super B) with revised specifications and increased weights, not least with maximum takeoff weight up to 833,000lb/378t (an increase from the earlier 755,000lb/333t); this marked the first true definitive framing to the 747 family. The -200's range would go up from just under 5,000mi to its ultimate range of 6,560mi, or nudging 12,150km.

Pan Am's early-build 747s (across line numbers 2 to 18) were upgraded to developed specification and Pan Am briefly cited them as -100A variants, but this was never an official Boeing tag.

The F for Freighter version saw the passenger windows deleted, weight saved from removing all passenger facilities (such as galleys and lavatories), a much stronger, cargo-bearing floor and freight-moving roller-conveyor mechanism fitted, and, of vital note, the forward-hinged nose cargo door (lifting) mechanism. Lufthansa operated the first one in Europe as D-ABYE from 1973 onwards. A later SF Special Freighter saw the side cargo door (the SCD kit) of the -200M Combi design added to converted ex-passenger airframes. These options added further to the 747's cargo abilities. Adding an SCD to a nose-opening freighter was also an option, just to confuse the airline enthusiast. The first true side cargo door (only) SF conversions were applied to two ex- American Airlines -100s in 1974 and then into service for 1975 with the legendary Flying Tigers. The SF conversion has since been applied to many earlier 747 airframes.

The -200C (Convertible) could be had with the upward-opening nose door of the freighter allied to the ability to revert to passenger operations – all passenger windows being retained except those close to the nose fuselage hinge line and two windows either side on the forward cabin. The freight-handling floor roller conveyor on the strengthened floor had to be removed for reversion to passenger accommodation. This was not a Boeing 'Quick Change' kit as seen on smaller airframes. World Airways flew the first -200C and 13 -200Cs were constructed. Adding a side cargo door to the rear fuselage really did boost this 747's adaptability and Iraqi Airways flew the first such conversion into service as early as 1976.

Power

With increases in thrust from the Pratt & Whitney engines and, soon, offerings of more powerful engines from General Electric and from Rolls-Royce, the -200 incorporated not just more power and range, it built in lots of new cabin features that customer experiences had created. The first Rolls-Royce RB211-524D-series-powered -200 service was British Airway's -200B G-BDXA in September 1976, with the 50,000lb-thrust engines that were soon added to the BA-200 fleet as a D-series upgrade.

An internally stretched upper deck with galley and cart-lift facility and, ten cabin windows per side, marked out the more versatile -200. Strangely, and confusingly, early -200s had been delivered with just three upper-deck windows per side (as with the -100) but -100s and early -200s could be modified to a ten-window configuration with a window modification kit.

Today, the oldest -200 left is N303TW, but the oldest -200B (preserved) with public access is ZS-SAN, the much-loved South African Airways *Lebombo*, now at Rand Aviation Museum in its final livery, having undertaken a stunning aerobatic display upon its arrival.

747-200E4B
An early and singular airframe USAF adaptation of the -200 airframe with airborne counter-measures equipment and revised structural items and an in-flight refuelling probe fitting. Ultimately, just three E4Bs were built. An ex-USAF -200 E4B dating from 1973 remains airworthy.

747-VC25A
The American 'Air Force One' operated by the USAF 89th Airlift Wing is based on a -200B but with many enhancements and tooling changes, notably a lower cargo deck entry door and step system. Also with in-flight refuelling, it has numerous classified features, ECAM and defence systems plus a medical centre and, of course, the Presidential, State Staff and Press cabins. Military use of a modified 747 airframe by the USAF saw two -VC25A airframes constructed amid the E4B specification. The -VC25A was to be the generic Air Force One 747-200 type, but strictly speaking that only applies to whichever airframe the president actually occupies. Serving from 1990, the -VC25A has a range of 7,800mi/12,600km with 70 passengers and underfloor freight. Of interest, the -VC25A contains double the amount of wiring compared to an airline-specification 747.

747 YAL-1A was the sole military 747 airframe adapted to airborne Laser Test status.

-200: Airline Details and KLM Magic

KLM Royal Dutch Airlines (Koninklijke Luchtvaart Maatschappij), founded in 1919, is a famous and key 747 operator. The airline originally took Pratt & Whitney-powered -200s in a white-top livery, and by October 1975 it had pioneered the GE CF6-50 engine on airline wings on the KLM -200B PH-BUH. It also deployed its spectacular bright-blue-topped livery design – that is unlikely to be bettered. Of note, in KLM configuration (and also with Qantas) was the option of a long galley layout on the right-hand side above the main forward cargo door – a specification that improved local structural strength above the large cargo door aperture.

KLM had always been a Douglas Company customer but could not ignore the 747. From its innovative -200SUD conversions through to its fleet of -300 and -400 equipment (notably with SCD/Combi configuration), KLM made the most of the Boeing options' list and made very successful use of the Combi concept across all its 747s. KLM also operated a 747F fleet.

Freighter versions, and even Combis with a forward passenger cabin, could in the cargo areas, dispense with internal cabin furnishing – ceilings and wall liners – which saved a lot of weight.

The -200M (or Combi) with large left-side rear cargo door and mixed/convertible cabin configuration was popular, again a KLM leader. Of interest was a 'converted' -200B SUD with 11 airframes cited for rebuild and stretched upper-deck conversions, the principal player being

Later Pratt & Whitney engine cowling attached to an SAA wing at Heathrow with -200s and -SPs behind. (Photo Author)

KLM. In Combi format, two passenger cabin options were available with two respective rear cargo-hold pallet options – you could mix and match seats to containers. A close maintenance eye had to be kept on that big rear cargo door and its constant use. Fuselage and door skin damage had to be monitored.

Lead -200 operator KLM initially had six -200s converted to later-SUD specification (aping the -300's appearance) in the early 1980s. More were to follow, but KLM's original P&W-engined -200 airframes were left unmodified. KLM operated post-1971-delivery -200Bs, then GE-powered post-1975 -200Bs and M fleet Combis. It latterly converted two ex-passenger -200 SUDs (prior-conversions) to cargo freighters, having previously confused things by converting several second-phase -200s to -300 SUD specification: KLM deployed the -300 and then the -400 from 1989: the -400M was a fantastic tool for KLM – not least because of its global racehorse transport service.

The -200's SUD modification kit added only two percent to the operating empty weight and yet added 10 percent in seating capacity – more if the SUD was configured with tight-pitched economy seats. A five percent fuel-consumption benefit on a seat-per-mile cost was the outcome. This project led to the eventual outcome of the short-lived -300 EUD variant. KLM Asia shared the KLM livery except for body and tail titling.

Union de Transports Aériens (UTA) of France took delivery of two converted -200SUD airframes. The airline operated 14 747s from 1979 to 1992 before it was absorbed by Air France. UTA was a -200M (Combi) fan with nearly half the fleet being so configured. UTA also flew three -200Fs and a fleet of -300Ms also marked up with historic Aeromaritime titles. One of these -300s – F-GETB – ended up as the Iranian Mahan Air airframe that was in service up to late 2015.

Alitalia (I-DEMA) had purchased the 747 for Italy via the -100 (three operated) with a mid-1970 arrival into the airline, but it really took to the -200B with 19 operated from 1971–2003, the later examples with GE powerplants. Several -200F airframes were operated by Alitalia, notably a converted airframe on a lease-back from Atlas Air (I-DEMW).

Scandinavian Airlines System (SAS) ran a fleet of very nicely kept -200s on polar routes and this service is often forgotten; we might say the same of the **Sabena** -100 and -200 fleet on its Africana and North Atlantic sectors out of Brussels – some being French F-registered rather than Belgian OO registered. This airline would latterly fly the -300 and -300M variants.

Cathay's Rolls-Royce -200s

After years of political battles with London, Hong Kong's Swire Group-owned Cathay Pacific Airways (CPA or CX coded) won traffic rights to and from the UK. After its L1011 Tristar years, it bought into the 747 in 1979 and chose an initial fleet that was subject to continuous upgrades. Cathay took nine -200Bs, three 200Fs, four -200SF and six -300s. Then came its 20 -400s, 14 -400BCFs and six -400Fs. The green-striped machines made a fine sight turning on the 47-degree sharp right turn into Hong Kong

Above: Qantas' Super B -200 in the earlier 'ochre' livery as the *City of Canberra* is delivered. (Qantas)

Left: KLM 747-400 in new blue and all polished up. Note the nose contours and windscreen designs. (Author)

Heavyweight
Lufthansa -200F
D-ABYU goes on up.
(Lufthansa)

Kai Tak under the famous Chequerboard Hill and onto the harbour runway. Cathay pioneered Rolls-Royce RB211-engined 747 flights of over 14 hours' duration across the Pacific with its 747s. On 8 October 2016, the last CX Cathay 747 passenger-spec airframe flight occurred, carrying the last of over 130 million Cathay 747 passengers over a 37-year operating period.

An older Cathay -300 slips into Kai Tak in style having made the 47-degree right-hand turn onto the runway. Super stuff from the Swire Group. (Author)

Korean Air became a major 200, -300 and -400 operator (with one -SP) but had an unfortunate (earlier) service accident record that required intervention. Latterly returning to global safety culture status, Korean Air has operated 55 of the earlier 747 models and has now added the -800i and -800F and proudly operates over a dozen of the ultimate 747s today. The airline was one of the last to retain the -400.

Virgin Atlantic (Virgin) was a latecomer to 747 operations yet built up a fleet of 16 -200s (including leased airframes) before moving on to the -400 (seven airframes) which appeared in a series of modern and individual liveries. Curiously, in 1990, Virgin's late-entry, sole -100 was G-VMIA as a leased -100 named *Spirit of Freddie* (latterly renamed *Miami Maiden*) but the airline's own initial -200 (G-VIRG) had arrived in 1984 as Virgin Atlantic's first widebodied aircraft and launched the airline's London Gatwick–Newark service to great fanfare: 1986, 1989 and 1990 would see arrivals into the fleet of used -200s. Regular, major livery design changes would be applied to the -200 and -400 fleets. Of interest, the sole Virgin -100 G-VMIA had also served with famous names such as American Airlines, Qantas and as the single airframe for Highland Express.

How many 747 fans know that the Virgin -200B G-VIRG equipped with Pratt & Whitney JT9Ds, flew non-stop from Hawaii to its British home via a great circular route when returning from maintenance in Australia? This airframe was one of the ex-Aerolineas Argentinas fleet from the 1980s and was Virgin's Maiden Voyager early flagship in operation from 1984 to 2001.

The 747 – notably the -200 – built the Virgin brand, alongside Branson, branding and individual design and slick marketing.

Corsair (International) was a key French 747 airline at second-tier high-density holiday operations which operated a superb and proud 747 fleet, culminating in its -400 operation. One airframe went beyond 123,000 flight hours (over double the 747 manufacturer's original estimated

Northwest -400 #6308 awaits its next uplift on a hot blue day. That red top helped air traffic spot the aircraft too. Cargo door open and last luggage to go in. (Photo Author)

Analogue excitement captured from the jump-seat on a Garuda -200 at sunrise on board the PK-GSE at FL37 at Mach 84. (Author)

flight hours) and still looked very well cared for. Corsair's operations saw 587 seats crammed into its later -400s for their holiday-flight configuration. This was even more seats than JAL or ANA on domestic 747-SR services. At one stage, the -400s wore a bright blue main livery during TUI ownership of Corsair, but a later, classier livery design was applied featuring sail motifs of great style. Twenty-three 747s flew in the Corsair 747 family from 1992 to mid-2020, with five -300s being ex-SIA. The 400s were ex-UAL and had appropriate registrations that included F-HSEX, F-HSUN, F-GTUI and F-HSEA. Perhaps most interesting of all was Corsair's single, lonely 747-SP which it flew from 1994 to 2002.

The Short One: 747-SP (1975 1987)

Special Performance (-SP) by name and special performance by nature, the SP was not quite a pocket rocket, but it was of higher performance, especially when fitted with Rolls-Royce RB211 engines, so it really was a hot ship. Qantas was the only airline to take the 747 – with the -SP – into the strict operating conditions of Wellington airfield, New Zealand, and its tough runway requirements. Qantas also inaugurated non-stop transpacific flights with their -SPs.

-SPs are special and none more so than a Qantas Rolls-Royce -SP like this one. (Qantas)

Quickly created on paper in 1972 to compete with the more economical three-engined DC-10 and L-1011 TriStar that had been cleared for long-haul and oceanic flights, the -SP was Boeing's answer to airline accountants and three-engined economy. The -SP was also the answer to tougher operational requirements and long-thin routes in airline jargon.

First design studies as a Short Body or Special Performance type were launched in 1972. The -SP first flew on 4 July 1975, before Pan Am service from March 1976 gave the airline a tool for routes deep into Europe and the Near East, direct from America's heartland as well as a more economical machine for transpacific and South American flights. New York–Tokyo was a key Pan Am -SP launch route. South African Airways pioneered its -SPs from 1976.

At this time Pan Am was still operating flights to the Iran of the US-backed Shah of Iran, with New York–Tehran a vital ultra-long-haul sector. The airline was also flying to India via a round-the-world routing through tropical operating conditions of hot-and-high type.

American Airlines operated two -SP airframes in silver finish on selected long-haul intercontinental routes. American leased in a TWA -SP, with TWA operating three -SPs itself. One TWA -SP (VP-BLK) and one Pan Am -SP (VQ-BMS) lived further lives with the Sands Corporation based in Las Vegas.

Air Namibia -SP roars out of Frankfurt en route to Africa. (Photo Author)

South African Airways -SPs were a speciality – as seen as a livery profile. (via Author)

747 Key -SP Operators

New deliveries and second-hand airframes as used deliveries:
Pan Am
Transworld Airlines (TWA)
United Airlines
American Airlines
Qantas (Rolls-Royce engined)
South African Airways
Saudia
Aerolineas Argentinas
Air China
CAAC
Korean Air
Iran Air
Iraq Airways
Syrian Arab Airlines

Royal/VIP/State -SP operators:
Brunei (Sultan VIP Flight)
Yemen VIP Flight
Oman Royal Flight
Saudi VIP Flight
Abu Dhabi Royal Flight (last -SP delivered 1987)

Further -SP second-hand airframe users:
Air Atlanta
Corsair
Mandarin Airlines
Cameroon Airlines
LuxAir
Air Malawi
Royal Air Maroc
Air Mauritius
Air Namibia
Trek Airways
Kazakhstan Airlines

At 47ft/14m shorter than a standard-length 747 fuselage, the -SP offered less passenger capacity but lower weight and longer range. It could also fly higher and had much-improved take-over and high-altitude performance to 43,000ft+, with some reputedly reaching nearly 45,000ft/13,700m.

The -SP was 176ft 9in/53.87m long – in comparison to the standard 747 length of 225ft 2in/68.63m. In order to regain longitudinal stability (moment arm), as aerodynamic yaw balance had been affected by the shortening, the SP featured a taller tailfin/empennage and longer-span tailplane/horizontal stabilizers with a 10ft or 3.5m increase. The wing flaps were also of simplified design which saved weight over the standard 747's triple-slotted flaps and heavy flap tracks and fairings. The highly efficient leading-edge devices were retained. Wing metal gauge was reduced in certain areas due to lower airframe weight and lower stresses.

A significant and often-overlooked major structural design change (of some expense to Boeing) was that the shorter front and rear fuselage sections meant that the upper-deck lobe now joined the main fuselage section further back on the body over the wing torsion box: this was further aft than in the 747-100 and -200. This led to structural re-engineering at this point and some investigations into the loading, pressurization patterns and torsional rigidity forces upon related fuselage structure above the wing box and body hoops. Of note, the number of main fuselage doors (as apertures) was reduced to increase local stiffness and accounted for lower passenger numbers in the cabin compared to the 400+-seater standard 747 body. Some long-body 747 airlines latterly tried this to squeeze in a handful of extra economy seats.

Despite being shorter and lighter, this was a still a heavy machine – at 700,000lb (320 ton) max takeoff weight, the standard range was just under 6,000mi at 5,850mi/10,800km. But with the right seat plan and Rolls-Royce engines, an -SP could exceed 6,600mi/12,318km.

Typical mixed-class (two classes) passenger seating was for 330 depending on layout. A First, Business and Economy Class configuration would lower the capacity to around 276 seats. However, a smaller Business Class cabin could allow for over 340 Economy Class seats. An all-economy -SP might seat nearly 400 passengers in a very tight seat pitch, but that would affect performance and range and perhaps be a self-defeating option. The reduced exits would also impact such density configuration. Early JT9D-powered -SPs were limited to less than 250 seats on some routes. The ultimate

Rolls-Royce 524D4-engined -SP had just on 52,000lbf/231kN of thrust per engine versus the Pratt & Whitney JT9D's lesser 46,950lbf/208.8kN. The -SP could get to a maximum speed of Mach 0.92 and flew above FL41 on transpacific sectors.

Despite all its advantages, the facts from the start were that the -SP would have higher seat-per-mile costs and lower yield. It also carried less freight under the floor. So, the savings in weight and size were real, but with operating costs still high. Nevertheless, this was a high-flying, smooth-riding 747 of great technical and route-planning interest. Adding powerful and economical Rolls-Royce RB211 500-series (finally as the 524-D4) engines really made the accountants smile – as well as the pilots.

Forty-five -SP airframes were built and seven remain in flying condition, with 15 in storage in varying conditions. As recently as 2016, Iran Air, despite sanctions, were still flying their venerable -SP – now grounded. The often-forgotten Korean Air -SP (HL7457) was operated from 1980–97, but then passed back to American ownership as a test-airframe last registered to Pratt & Whitney Canada in 2020 as C-GTFF.

Also often forgotten is the sole Corsair -SP, F-GTOM or Tom, which flew with the French carrier from late 1994 to late 2002 as the single French -SP example of significance. This airframe was flown to Chateauroux 20 years ago for disposal, yet (to date) remains unscrapped and a remarkable static tribute to the French -SP operation. The airframe is 44 years old

The -SP also found favour as a VIP, royal and corporate machine as well as the famous airborne telescope for the Stratospheric Observatory for Infared Astronomy (SOFIA) with its special observatory door in place of a normal main deck cargo hatch.

An ex-SAA -SP is preserved in South Africa. SAA flew their -SP ZS-SPA direct from Boeing Field Seattle to Cape Town on its record-breaking delivery flight in 1976 and less than a month later inaugurated a direct flight to Europe. SAA had a scare when ZS-SPF (on short joint wet-lease share with Air Mozambique) experienced an engine failure on climb-out from Maputo. The adjacent engine was also damaged and a fire broke out close to the wing tanks. An immediate forced landing of great skill saved the lives of all on board.

An interesting -SP flight was the Pan Am '50' flight code of 28 October 1977 that celebrated the airline's anniversary by flying around the world in an attempted 50 hours. The flight actually took 54 hours and routed San Francisco–London Heathrow–Cape Town–Auckland–San Francisco. Both polar points were traversed and Admiral R. Byrd was duly tributed in the air.

Aerolineas Argentinas operated a single -SP (ex-Braniff) for several years and it ranged far and wide in superb style.

The famous 1985 China Airlines Flight 006 'aerobatic' -SP flight accident incident 'roll' and high Mach dive through over 30,000 feet is cited earlier in the book but bears a further brief mention in terms of its proof of design for the vital strength of the 747 airframe.

The rare Korean -SP in flight. Note the taller fin. (Boeing)

747-300 Classic

A longer upper deck or top, and two extra emergency exists on the upper deck defined the -300 iteration of the classic 747. The removal of the spiral staircase and new straight staircase, better aerodynamics over the aircraft's upper section, and a number of engineering modifications created the -300 extended upper-deck 747 – the EUD in classification terms (the SUD was a 1980 precursor -200 conversion-type name, later to become the -300-design signifier from 1982). Of interest, JAL ordered a late -100 with a stretched or extended upper deck but then focused on a special version of -300 EUD for domestic cycles.

In the -300 the longer upper-body lobe created not only significant structural changes, including fuselage hoops as far back as the wing, it also changed the aerodynamics of the 747 for the better – adding 0.01 to the top Mach speed. The longer lobe with flatter side walls aided airflow transition down the fuselage length and reduced aerodynamic noise.

October 1982 saw the first -300 flight and the type entered service in March 1983 with Swissair.

Eighty-one -300 airframes are cited in official figures with 56 being passenger versions, and 22 the Combi configuration -300M series. But we must recall that KLM converted six of its existing (later) -200B airframes at vast expense to stretched (cited by KLM as SUD) upper-deck configuration during major maintenance schedules at the Seattle plant as a conversion programme. Later, new -300EUD Combis entered the KLM fleet. JAL used four of its -300 SRs on short-haul routes. UTA of France was a niche -300 operator and tagged theirs with a Big Boss logo on the upper fuselage, latterly added to their -400s. These were the airframes that flew to the French Pacific territories on a weekly ultra-long-haul sector.

Curiously, BA did not take the -300. The last new -300 went to Belgium's Sabena in 1989. The -300M mixed configuration proved the most popular -300 iteration. The last operating base of the -300 was in Russia and Iran. Nigerian operators had actually used the -300 in various guises. Pakistan International Airlines (PIA) flew the last mainline international -300 operations into 2015 using ex-Cathay Pacific airframes on lease. Russia's Transaero also dabbled in -300 operations and would do likewise with the -400.

Key -300 operators:
Swissair
KLM
Qantas
Sabena
UTA
Air France
JAL
Egypt Air
PIA

The -300 was a short-lived programme that offered a small fiscal benefit to the 747 operator. It was not without merit but was to be eclipsed by the much better economics, aerodynamics and electronics of the -400 that came into being from 1985. The -300 was also seen in the colours of many second-tier holiday airlines and others. Of note Corsair, Excel/XL Airways and Air Atlanta Icelandic deployed -300s, but so too did GMG Airlines of Bangladesh. The last new -300 delivery was as late as September 1990 with OO-SGD for Sabena.

The -300 was developed as work began at Boeing on the -300A (Advanced). This became the heavily revised new -400.

New Digital Age: -400
The late 1980s design highlight was the new -400 with revised wing aerodynamics and airframe systems and efficiencies, notably the electronic flight deck and two-pilot crew operation. A tail fuel tank was offered. The -300's launch airline, Swissair, chose to abandon Boeing and did not order the -400. Neither did the smaller Sabena. Many of the major 747 Classic devotees

KLM -SUD in blue at Schiphol about to head off to JFK on the KL 641 service as the GE engines warm up. (Author)

KLM revised its blue in the new millennium but kept the vital hue. Here the -400 Melbourne awaits pushback at Schiphol. Historic KLM emotion – as usual. (Author)

did option the -400 and it became the most popular and reliable long-haul tool in the airline world across the 1990s and was still being purchased new after 2000.

-400 had its first flight on 29 April 1988 and was even more popular with pilots than the earlier 747s; its ability to sort itself out, avoid trouble or deal with trouble, was legendary. You just had to watch out for the longer wings and the risks of scraping a winglet in a crosswind.

Key differences included the twin crew, glass TV-screened digital electronic (EFIS-type) flight deck and computerized flight management systems. A revised wing of 211ft compared favourably to the 195ft 8in of the previous models and the addition of the winglets to tune tip-vortices actually added a small lift component. The wing root was improved in aerodynamic flow terms and other airflow tweaks were incorporated. The weight increase to 870,000lb in the -400 was up from the -100's 710,000lb; a significant increase in fuel capacity was to 57,285 gallons – 10,000 more than the -100's.

On 4 February 1989 the -400 entered service life at Northwest Airlines as launch customer. As early as September 1989, the first -400 Combi flew with launch airline KLM. BA, LH, SQ and QF all soon followed by 1991. SIA made marketing magic out of its 'Mega-Top' -400s.

-400 went on to many upgrades with notable new cabin and seat designs for the new long-haul luxury age. Its safety, stability, range and strength made it the new Queen of the airways. At the forced and premature end of blue-riband -400 operations in 2020, the Spanish Wamos Air -400 fleet was used for repatriation flights by several authorities in 2020. Lufthansa ranged far and wide with -400s to recover German citizens. In late 2020, Russia's Rossiya airline was running regular -400 passenger services.

Developments

-400D: Launched in the early 1990s, with capacity for up to 568 seats in two-class configuration or over 600 in a tight all-economy 30-inch seat pitch, the -400D (Domestic) does what it says on the tin: -400D is lighter, stronger, has less fuel tankage but more seats; it was a specific outcome of the 747's earlier SR/BSR/BSR/EUD variations created principally for the high-density Japanese internal city–city

Looking towards the front of the extended upper deck, this really was the height of 747 style – as seen in the lovely Lufthansa cabin. (Lufthansa)

Lufthansa's -400 *Kiel* being towed to the stand for service. Lufthansa spends a lot of time and money keeping its airframes shiny. This is the less-than-popular new livery design. (Lufthansa)

market for JAL and ANA respectively. The winglets were removed and extra seats and windows were seen on the internally extended upper deck minus a galley and cart-lifts. Nineteen -400Ds were constructed and ANA operated the last one in March 2014.

-400ER: This was another Boeing special that became another Qantas one-off type. With increased range, higher weights, stronger undercarriage and new engines, it was a long-hauler for a specific transpacific route. This was a near-6,000-mile-range 747 at 5,700mi/9,200km. There was even the option of two 3,200-gallon cargo-hold-mounted extra fuel tanks. But such options were declined except in some later freighter iterations such as the -400ERF. The -400 horizontal stabilizer fuel tank would provide enough c.g. without adding to the complex fuel transfer mechanics.

Crucially, the -400ER added 500mi/805km more range to the standard -400. Given the right winds and cruising altitudes, this could be stretched a touch further. Less range required meant a payload increase of the order of 15,000lb/6,850kg. The freighter version as the -400ERF was launched as late as 2001 which means that, unless overused, such airframes remain competitive. Air France put their -400ERFs to good use. Some 40 -400 ERFs have been built.

Qantas managed to run from Melbourne to Los Angeles and the wind-critical return sector with its -400ERs: a significant achievement.

Above all, -400ER hit the magical 910,000lb/412,769kg maximum weight with an impressive payload of nearly 250,000lb at 248,6000lb/112,770kg. The later -800F had more payload volume but less ultimate range than its -400 predecessor. The freighter variant as -400ERF was a rarer airframe.

747-400BCF: BCF stands for Boeing Converted Freighter and repurposed ex-passenger configuration airframes into freighters. Launched in early 2005, this 747 type first took to the air with Cathay Pacific Cargo in late 2005.

747-400BSDF: A Bedek -400 freighter passenger-to-freight/cargo airframe conversion from Israeli specialist Aerospace Industries. EVA and Air China have received such types.

-400LCF: Boeing launched its special, non-production model slab-sided Large Cargo Freighter with very expensive new fuselage toolings in early 2004. Four were built – by Boeing contractors – and the last conversion first flew in 2010. Airframe component transport lay behind the LCF's conception. This unique design featured a full-length double deck with lobed and extended fuselage side walls to facilitate wide cargos, notably 787 sections, and had a taller 747-SP-type tailfin/rudder added for better directional control.

April 2005 saw the last passenger-specification -400 delivery, to China Airlines. Upon retirement, British Airways had more than one -400 with in excess of 90,000 airframe hours and one with 103,000 hours – so the airline got its money's worth.

New Age 747: -800

In 2006, Boeing scoped out plans for the -800 which was a major redesign with a new wing and a fuselage of longer length with two plugs (ahead of and aft of the wing box) and featuring significant systems and structural changes. Delivery was cited for 2011 but -800 services arrived a touch later.

A 442-ton (975,000lb) monster originally mooted way back in 2006, the new, -800 Intercontinental and the -800 Freighter are expensive but worthwhile final tweaks of a 50-year-old design, but by no means inefficient just because they lack tons of carbon fibre or marketing bling. A near 15 percent saving in seat-per-mile

Left: Inside Boeing. The 747's Sections 41 and 42 are mated to the main wing box by being hoisted through the air. (Boeing)

Below: Boeing's best, the -800I, is captured in-build as the national flag reminds workers of the achievement. The tailfin has yet to be winched in. (Boeing)

operating costs over the -400 was a major achievement. Fuel efficiency improvements exceeded 12 percent over the -400 and more than 20 percent over the -200. Range went up to 7,730 miles whereas the early -100 flew 4,620 miles. The -800 saved over two gallons of fuel per mile in the cruise compared to the original 747, so -800 gets better miles per gallon. In terms of the 747's specific fuel consumption, the -800 has made huge strides towards economic efficiency. More thrust, more fuel tankage and more maximum gross takeoff weight (MGTW) all add to the -800's operating excellence.

-800-type ratings were little different from those of -400 and the handling characteristics not too dissimilar. Structural loadings varied only slightly and the reinforced floor carried the same loadings per square foot or square meter.

Compared to the -400, the -800 could (via its fuselage stretch) offer room for 51 more passengers in totally new cabin architecture and, in the freighter version, would add 16 percent more cargo volume. The new cabin designs with more comfort were key -800 features, and an all-economy, high-density -800 might seat nearly 600 passengers.

The -800 featured a new wing aerofoil and planform shape of even greater aerodynamic efficiency at the wing root and wingtip. Of note, the flaps were simpler and lighter than the 747's original triple-slotted panels. The new wing aerofoil section and raked outer span added to the lift components (CL), reducing the need for the triple-slotted flaps effect. Less lift-induced drag stems from the ellipsoid, curved wingtips – not winglets as seen on -400.

New GE (GenEx) engines of great high-bypass-ratio efficiency, and structural and avionics refinements, really did deliver a viable new chapter in the 747's amazing history. Boeing's research test pilot was veteran Tom Imrich who had flown all variants of the 747 and led the -400 and

New engine casing designs with chevron-shaped edges to the turbine casing reduced noise via an aerodynamic streaming effect upon the local airflow. Note also the -800's revised pylon design that allowed a deeper engine by raising the mounting point upwards. (Boeing)

-800I, the new flagship, with decades of service to come, seen alongside the 787. (Boeing)

the -800 development flying. Rolls-Royce or Pratt & Whitney engine options were offered, but the serrated-edge turbine casing design was vital to -800's noise-reduction ability of a 30 percent smaller noise footprint.

-800 is 18.3 feet longer than -400, almost 250 feet long, with a redesigned aerofoil, revised wing-root aerodynamics and the deletion of winglets and use of ellipsoid

British Airways -800F slips the bonds of a wet Washington State runway on its delivery flight. (Boeing)

-800F reverted to the long-abandoned short upper-deck lobe and ignored the EUD configuration. Lead customer Cargolux gets going from the Boeing plant. (Boeing)

extended-span wingtip. Also deployed was the first use of saw-tooth engine nacelles exhaust vanes to reduce noise and improve airflow vortices. Total -800I fuel capacity is a startling 64,225 US gallons.

The updated electronic flight management system no longer needed a floppy disc (and a monthly recode!) that had endured on the -400.

The -800F with its near 150-ton payload ability flew first in February 2010, and the 800I (Intercontinental) passenger liner first flew in March 2011. The first in-service revenue flight of the -800I was not until the summer of 2012 and sales did not really build for some time. Lufthansa made something special out of its -800I, while Korean Air and Air China tweaked theirs into blue-riband cruisers. The Air China -800I featured fewer seats (at 375) than possible (470) but offered a four-class cabin and great luxury for long-range flying. Russia's Transaero ordered two -800s but these were not delivered due to the airline's fiscal status and ironically were to be slated for conversion for the US Government presidential flight.

The main structural and visual note of the freighter variant -800F is the use of the old, shorter -100/-200-style upper-deck lobe, whereas -800I keeps the long or extended -300/-400-type upper fuselage lobe. Over 150 -800 airframes have been ordered. CargoLux and then Nippon Cargo Airlines became the major operators. Cathay Pacific Cargo also optioned several -800Fs. The passenger variants bring up the rear with a smaller percentage of the fleet – which may hit 50 airframes out of the current total of 154 delivered/ordered. The decision to end the -800 production programme was taken later in 2020 off the back of the Covid pandemic and its commercial effects on the airline transport business.

More recent -800F operators include Air Bridge Cargo, Atlas Cargo, UPS, Polar Air Cargo, Silk Way, Qatar Cargo and Cargo

The nose-loading Freighter design has stood the test of time across the five decades; what a piece of equipment, one unrivalled by an Airbus. (Boeing)

Logic. The Qatari Amiri Flight took three VIP-configured -800s but recently put one up for sale. Oman also took the VIP-specification -800, as did the Saudi Crown and the Royal Brunei Government.

747 VC-25B will provide a USAF lead airframe for years to come after the VC25A -200 airframe is retired as Air Force One, with VC-25B being based on a modified, unused -800 airframe having been undelivered.

Above: Cathay Pacific Cargo rises as their -800F is captured on climb-out. 'Gear up please' will be called soon. (Boeing)

Right: On board the -800 as the flight-test crew make ready amid the digital environment with good old-fashioned hardcopy checklists! (Boeing)

Below: 747s worked hard even with premier carriers. Sadly, BA let this -400 get a bit scruffy and she needed a respray to the Landor livery. (Author)

747: Serving the World

The final BA 747 livery seen in storage due to the Covid pandemic. (Author)

The sheer success of the 747 design concept was underlined by the global airlines – large and small – that made the 747 their own marketing and operational tools. Major new carriers emerged from their 747 eras. First there came the historic legacy airlines such as KLM (see chapter 2), Lufthansa, Qantas and BOAC, then emerged the new players such as Singapore Airlines and others.

BOAC to BA: Five Decades of Speedbird 747 Operations

British Airways (BA) operated up to 71 747 airframes at peak usage, and 101 across its total 747 fleet service life. At the same time, the airline also ran Pratt & Whitney-powered -100s, Rolls-Royce RB 211 D4-series re-engined -200s (from September 1976), and later RB211-524G/H/T-powered -400s. BA's Boeing customer code was -36, hence its 747 fleet's -136, -236 and -436 codings. BA repainted three -400s in retro liveries – G-BYGC, G-BNLY and G-CIVB – and these (notably the BOAC-liveried example) provided a stunning 747 tribute for the airline prior to the service withdrawal exercise.

BA's fleet stemmed from its British Overseas Airways Corporation (BOAC) origins prior to this 1974 merger with British European Airways to form the new British Airways. BOAC had its roots in Imperial Airways and had no actual linkage with the 1930s airline known as British Airways which was an entirely separate airline transport company in the1930s. BA's recent claims to be 100 years old are thus tenuous, to put it mildly.

A BA -400 seen in the cruise as the captain works the numbers in the FMS/NAV portal. (Author)

The BOAC fleet introduced in April 1970 were all Pratt & Whitney powered and had the underpowered sensitive JT9 D3 engines, but they did boast a stunning blue and white livery with a golden BOAC Speedbird emblem on the tailfin. These original aircraft (G-AWNA, G-AWNO) were repainted in the new BA colours in stages of hybrid livery and titles in 1974/5. Several ex-Qantas -138s and ex-Lufthansa -230s were also to be acquired alongside the direct BA orders for new 747 airframes. The last ex-BOAC -100 left BA service in 1999

A rare sight, the BA 100 BOAC retro livery on G-BYGC, seen in company with the Red Arrows. Note the -400's long-podded Rolls-Royce engines. (Author)

and the last BA -200 went in 2002, both types having been repainted in the Landor livery. BOAC/BA had operated 19 of the -100s in total, adding 26 -200s and latterly 57 -400s. BA terminated -400 operations in the summer of 2020.

British Caledonian (BCAL) and its wonderful and sadly missed 747 fleet (of one leased -100 via Aer Lingus and five -200s) was absorbed into BA in 1988. Prior to that, the BCAL 747s with lion rampant on the tailfin roamed the world with great service – a distinct chapter in British 747 operations, of which the London Gatwick–Hong Kong service was a highlight. The BCAL -200 airframes came from respected earlier operators such as Lufthansa, Royal Jordanian and Wardair.

Of note, the ex-Lufthansa -200 D-ABYG was to become BCAL's *Mungo Park* as G-BJXN, then to be absorbed into the BA fleet. BCAL performed innovative rebuild work on its venerable 747s, including major structural work on key main fuselage structures. BCAL's -100 G-BDPZ served the London Gatwick–Houston route.

Caledonian as a brand was latterly reborn inside the BA fleet as a dedicated charter holiday brand with a stunning livery of blue and gold design. Several original BCAL 747s served in BA colours as well as the later Caledonian Airways blue and gold. Of note, the 1971-built ex-SAS -200 *Ivar Viking* served with Caledonian Airways as G-BMGS (via BA) from May 1989 as *Loch Ness*. This venerable (and much-rebuilt) machine, which once served Nigeria Airways, latterly joined the Virgin Atlantic fleet from BA as G-VOYG *Shady Lady*.

BA and R-R
Being British, BA launched the Rolls-Royce RB211-524 on the 747-200 wing as early as 1987. The RB211-powered 747 used

End of days. BA -400 tailfin and rear fuselage detail in storage at Cotswold Airport prior to Air Salvage International having to perform a sombre task. (Author)

between 7–9 percent less fuel than the existing Pratt & Whitney 747 engine (JT9D) and was soon chosen by Qantas, South African Airways and Cathay Pacific for ultra-long-haul transpacific operations.

The RB211-524 C-series increased thrust from 51,500lbf/229kN to 53,000lbf/240kN in the much-favoured -524D-series. The 524G-series engines on the -400 had offered 58,000lbf/260kN, eventually to hit 60,000lbf as the -524H-series. Pratt & Whitney had, by the 1980s, responded to the RB211 family, with its PW2000 engine and claimed to better the Rolls-Royce RB211-535 engine but not the RB211-524-G/H/HT developments. But Pratt & Whitney soon came up with the PW4053/4056 engine of 56,000lbf/252.4kN thrust – optioned notably by Singapore Airlines, but not by BA.

In 1998, BA created its -400 hybrid project where, among its then near 50-strong 747 fleet, a proportion of the newer -400s would receive a standardized RB211 524G/H retrofitted with the core of the larger Trent engine as the RB211-524 G/HT.

Interestingly, BA could, with minor modifications to oil pipes and thrust reverser configuration, also use the RB211-524 – seen on its 767-300s as spare engines for the 747-400 fleet – as the two engines were very similar, but it could not swap such engines from other airframes – and especially not the lower-powered RB211-535C variant used on its 757 fleet. L1011 Tristar 500s had also used the RB211 in the BA fleet in the 1980s.

Curiously, because the T-series-modified RB211-524 did not differ in thrust rating from the -524 G/H variants, these modified T-series engines with their Trent high-pressure turbines, combustor and compressor, could be mix-and-matched on the wing with non-modified -524 G/H engines – which seemed rather incredible, incurring no airframe or pilot-operating penalties. The T-series engines were each a significant 325kg lighter, had two percent better fuel economy and aided long-haul operations, notably in hot-and-high runway conditions.

BA retired its 30+-year-old -100 fleet from 1998. Two BA -200s (G-BDXL and G-BMGS) had even operated in full British Airtours markings for BA's holiday operation fleet with high-density seating. BA also owned a -200F freighter with the appropriate registration of G-KILO, but unwisely sold it.

In this era BA also leased in and bought various 747 airframes with very differing engine choices and cabin configurations to the BA standard customer type – as in -136, -236 and -436. BA never operated the -300. Later BA-400s featured varying seating plans including a high-capacity J/ Business Class 86-seat/57 layout known as Super High-J, High-J or Mid-J (still with the unpopular eight seats across), with a smaller Economy Class cabin and just 291–275–337 seats respectively in total for all classes – perhaps the lowest ever -400 accommodation figure.

2020 saw the final years of BA 747 service to every corner of the globe in a range of great liveries and configurations. At the end, one of BA's -400s (G-CIVN) had an incredible 103,000+ hours on its airframe but BA's G-CIVD had 115,276 flying hours on the clock – approaching *double* Boeing's original 747 design-life estimate. G-CIVD had flown 50 million miles and performed 13,365 flights.

BA's 747 had style, especially in the Landor livery (1984–97), and who can forget launching out of Heathrow over Windsor Castle in a 17-degree climb with noise abatement ignored and the upgraded RR 524s screaming their cores out to lift the champagne-filled cruiser into the clouds at maximum allowed full power boost – an amazing sound and experience amid the wail of those pulsating engines and fan blades. BA became the largest operator of the -400. Sadly, unlike other airlines, it succumbed to a corporate mindset and refused a 747 farewell tour or celebration when it prematurely retired the fleet, and in doing so alienated its own fan base.

Cathay Pacific, Air New Zealand and Qantas had mixed-type -400-engined variants with Rolls-Royce -524s, or alternatively the GE engine option. 747 operators who chose the Rolls-Royce RB211series from new, included:

Air New Zealand -200, -400
British Airways -200, -400
Cathay Pacific -200. -300, -400
Qantas -200 -300 -400, -SP
Saudia -200, -300, -SP
Malaysian -400

Other airlines and cargo carriers also leased in or purchased second-hand Rolls-Royce-powered 747 airframes. Some commentators expressed surprise that Lufthansa, with its ultra-long-haul routes, notably to South America and Asia, did not choose the powerful, yet economical, Rolls-Royce engines.

Lovely Lufthansa scenery at the Flughafen Frankfurt Am Main. A 747-400 trundles out to the runway. A stunning 747 memory. (Lufthansa)

Pratt & Whitney and General Electric engines were seen on most other -400s of the 1990s. Northwest Orient, United, Malaysian, Singapore Airlines, Lufthansa and many others chose such powerplant options.

Qantas 747s – a Beloved Fleet

The Queensland and Northern Territories Aerial Services (QANTAS) was a 747 customer across five decades and, having previously got Boeing to create its unique Qantas-spec 707-138 shortbody, long-range machines, would create a unique ER variant of the -400, as well as to operate Rolls-Royce RB211-powered -SPs. The Qantas 747s were hugely popular with Australian flight and cabin crews and with travelling Australians. 747 in QF colours were part of the nation's modern heritage across five decades. Remember, Qantas was an all-747 airline at one stage.

Qantas operated its early P&W-engined fleet, then went all R-R-engined and then created its unique -400 ER machines, but, contrary to the airline's previous Rolls-Royce long-haul engine choice, specified the new advanced General Electric engines in their long core cowlings for the -400ERs. Qantas also bought in three used -400 airframes with GE CF6-80C2B5/F-series engines (with increased fan diameter) and nearly 60,000lbf/263kN of thrust, so the fleet mix got more complex and the costs went up. Interestingly, the 747 ER/ERF could use GE CF6 engines or the later, longer Pratt & Whitney 4062-series engines.

Intriguingly, Qantas had waited for the -200B model of the 747 (operating 25) had latterly leased in a -100 model from Aer Lingus in 1987 and again in 1989 to cope with increased demand. A -200C was also leased.

Qantas's peak with its 747 operations was in 2000 when it operated a fleet of

Emotion at Sydney Kingsford Smith as the Qantas -400 VH-OJJ runs up to the stand in front of the author at work. Aussie Blue and Qantas quality. (Photo Author)

Above: A spotless Rolls-Royce RB211-524 G/H-series on the wing at Qantas. (Author)

Far left: Slats seen deployed on the outer section of a -400 series. Boeing's experience developing the 727's wing design transferred into the 747 high-lift devices. (Author)

Left: 747 multiple-rudder design seen at deflection on a KLM -400. Best to keep the rudder ratio device well maintained. (Author)

38 747s across five variants including the two very special -SP long-range machines with advanced Rolls-Royce engines. That fleet included 25 747-400s, six -300s, two remaining -200Bs and two very rarely cited -200 Combis (leased). The airline had in totality exceeded 60 747 airframes (owned or leased) across its 747 operating decades.

In 2020, post-Covid, Qantas prematurely retired its 747 passenger fleet but did retain its two leased freighter airframes. One Qantas -400ER would go to Rolls-Royce for use as an engine-test airframe.

Ansett Airlines was a long-established domestic Australian airline (1935–2002) which entered the 747 age with a fleet of leased-in -300 airframes. Ansett operated eight -300s, one of which was a -300M. Then it leased a fleet of four -400s, these being of ex-SIA ownership. For a few short years the unusually marked Ansett fleet provided an alternative Aussie -400 lifestyle, only to be ended by corporate history.

Lufthansa operated 61 747s across its type history and was the first non-U.S. airline to receive a 747. The airline used the 747 from the -100 first delivered in March 1970, the -200 from 1972, the Freighter from 1973, the -400 from September 1989, through to the -800 post-2013. The -300 was sidestepped by the German flag carrier yet Lufthansa was a major global force in the 747 fleet history despite the airline's later Airbus–European Union affiliations. Lufthansa subsidiary **Condor** took up several ex-Lufthansa mainline 747s early on in the 747 Classic story.

Lufthansa took a small fleet of -100s – grabbing 747 Boeing airframe line number 12 very early indeed (as D-ABYA) – from February 1970, then 26 of a mixed -200/M/F fleet across the 1970s–1980s. It was the -200 that Lufthansa used to create its high-quality safety and service hallmark. Today Lufthansa still retains a fleet of eight -400s (from ten), these being later-build (1997–2002) airframes. Like KLM, Lufthansa's wonderful livery design stood the test of time and yet was replaced by a hated, bland corporate branding exercise in recent years – hence the -800s wearing this livery – although the retro-livery effect as applied to a -800I looked superb. Sadly, Lufthansa had an early-service -100 fatal accident in 1974 but has since enjoyed an enviable safety record. Nineteen -800s now form the main fleet and several late-build -400s remain.

Expertly maintained by the airline (not at cheaper outsourcing) across the decades, Lufthansa's 747s always found eager second-hand buyers and operators. One of Lufthansa's premier 747 flights has been the Frankfurt–Santiago de Chile service across the South Atlantic and the Andes, a wonderful high-quality experience of global legend. Lufthansa 747 operations were rightly often regarded as best in class.

Air France also got on board the Boeing 747 bandwagon early in 1970 with airframe line number 19 (as F-BPVA). With -100s from 1971, by 1974 the airline was taking

Above: Classic 747 fins adorned with the trademark flying kangaroo on the ramp at Sydney. (Author)

Right: LH -400 *Schleswig-Holstein* rotates out of Frankfurt in a great airline moment. Note outer wing flex as the wing loading goes up. (Photo Lufthansa)

the 200 and, of note, three -200F airframes with GE engines. The first -200F arrived in 1974; the third had arrived by 1979 for Air France Cargo. In total Air France operated 73 examples of the 747 airframe and made a big mark with its -400s, the last of which left the carrier in January 2016. All achieved high cycles and high flying hours with the usual -400 reliability and efficiency.

Japan Airlines

Japan Airlines (JAL) had over 90 747 airframes in its fleet at its peak – at one stage leading the airline pack and having operated 103 747 airframes in totality. This included the special, high-density, short-range -100SR, the -100BSR and the very rare -100BSRSUD (Stretched Upper Deck) which seated 563 in total. At the beginning of the 1990s, JAL operated a 747 fleet-mix ranging from -100, -100SR/SUD through to over 40 -400s (domestic versions having 546 seats). JAL's daily non-stops from Tokyo to Moscow, Paris and London became world famous – as did its polar flights via Anchorage which had been carved out by JAL's superb Douglas DC-8 fleet in competition with the SAS DC-8 polar route.

Eire's Aer Lingus 747 Story

Ireland's national carrier provided an interesting chapter in the 747 story. Aer Lingus had an enviable operating and maintenance record and went on from operating the likes of BAC 1-11, Boeing 707, 737 and 747, to the later Airbus types. Famous Aer Lingus senior pilot Captain R.G. 'Bud' Bryce was the only Irish pilot to have flown Concorde (out of Toulouse) and was a key Irish Boeing and Airbus trainer and pilot.

Aer Lingus's first 747 was the Pratt & Whitney-powered -100, EI-ASI *St Padraig*, which arrived on 6 March 1971 when the airline took delivery in a lovely white-and-green-striped livery.

EI-ASJ was the airline's second -100 airframe and was leased out – and saw service with East African Airways, British Airways and British Caledonian. It is also reputed to have briefly worn Air Siam

stickers on a short wet lease. Like its stable mate, -ASJ ended up being sold off to a Nigerian operator.

EI-BED was the airline's third 747 and wore the second, green top Aer Lingus Shamrock livery. It was in fact a superbly maintained ex-Lufthansa airframe and just under a decade old. Underutilized, it was quickly leased out, notably to Air Algérie, and also to LAN Chile. Other lessees included Qantas and Air Jamaica. EI–BED flew many miles for Qantas and was a later -100 survivor in the Australian fleet. Aer Lingus also leased in a used 747-100 from Alitalia in the form of I-DEME for a short period, to cover major maintenance work on its own 747 fleet.

Aer Lingus terminated its niche 747 operations in October 1995. This drew the curtain on a 25-year operating history of a tiny 747 fleet operation yet one which offered high standards, great service and

Above: -800 of
Lufthansa D-ABYA
lands in classic repose.
(Lufthansa)

Below: Singapore
Airlines -400 in
company with other
airframes on a hot day
at Sydney.
(Author)

a global reach. Those in the know knew
that Dublin to Boston or New York and
beyond on an Aer Lingus 747 was a great
experience.

Singapore Airlines and the Big Top & Mega Top

Singapore Airlines (SIA), born from
Malaysia Singapore Airlines and its de
Havilland Comet fleet, became a Boeing
fan with its own SIA 707 fleet. From 1973
onwards, SIA operated the -200B variant
(as 212B) of the 747 in a fleet of 25 -200B
airframes. The fleet included two -200BSFs,
one -200ACM and three -200Fs. SIA's last
-200 left the passenger fleet in 1994 to be
replaced by the -300EUD and its Big Top

marketing-slogan livery. Twenty-two of the
-300s were at SIA including two -300SFs,
one -300M and one -300SF.

SIA then purchased 61 versions of the
-400 (as Mega Top) passenger airframes
but which also included the mixed fleet
of nine -400BCFs, 11 -400FSCDs and
(briefly) one -400BDSF. This made SIA the
largest -400 operator at one time in the
-400's history. The cargo fleet of -400s were
entitled Mega-Arks.

Constantly upgraded, featuring the
latest cabin and flight-deck upgrades, the
young fleet carved a significant reputation
for Singapore Airlines on a global network
rivalled by few regional competitors. The
famous Raffles Class has become Business
Class. SIA remains at the forefront of the
quality airline offering, but sadly it said
goodbye to the 747 and became an Airbus
devotee, despite operating 777s as well.

Egypt Air operated the -200 SU-GAK (as
a Swissair lease), and then the -300 as
SU-GAL and SU-GAM from 1983 onwards,
with SU-GAM in service to 2005.

Pakistan Airlines operated the -200B on
its flagship international routes from 1976
onwards – initially using two ex-TAP of
Portugal airframes on lease, followed by
six more -200s from varied sources, but
only two were new factory-order airframes.
It then operated a series of second-hand
-300s, notably the ex-Cathay Pacific
airframes.

Qatar Airways operated a small but
financially vital fleet of passenger and
cargo 747s as -100 and -200 airframes that
were its post-1995 key widebodies prior
to its expansion. The story of Qatari -SP
(A7-ABM) is a complicated tale of usage.
More recently two -800Fs have worked in
the Qatari cargo fleet.

All Nippon Airways (ANA)

ANA was to become a major 747-200
operator and its blue-and-white-hued 747s
made a fine contrast to JAL's traditional
red and white livery. Founded in the 1950s
from its roots as a helicopter transport
company, ANA operated British and
American types of aircraft but became

an early Boeing 727 customer, which led ANA to the mighty 747 via an L-1011 fleet diversion. ANA's 747 story began with the -100SRs in 1976 on domestic Japanese routes and then expanded into -200Bs. ANA's international 747 operations began in 1986 on transpacific services to the USA and the Pacific Rim. By 1990 ANA was serving Europe and New York, giving JAL some stiff competition. The ANA -200s were the fleet mainstay to 2005, after which the -400/-400D fleet took over. The ANA -400D seated 569 in high-density configuration.

South American 747s: Aerolineas Argentinas, Avianca, VIASA, and VARIG all provided South Atlantic route -100, -200B and -300 coverage for decades in an often-ignored chapter of 747 excellence.

Aerolineas Argentinas tried to lease a Delta -100 airframe in 1975 but failed, yet operated a 747 from 1977 with a sole -200 (as LV-MLO). A sister-shop LV-OPA served 23 years with the Argentine carrier. Twelve more 747s were acquired to include the -400. Initially the -200s were bought direct from Boeing as new airframes; seven more 747s of used status were then purchased or leased. All were well maintained and one was sold off and then formed the nucleus of the emerging Virgin Atlantic 747 fleet. LV-OHV was the rare bird that was the unique Aerolineas Argentinas -SP, being an ex-Braniff airframe. The -SP served a decade with Aerolineas Argentinas prior to ending up as a Qatar Airways machine – then to the Yemen State flight where it was destroyed in a non-accident event – a firefight at Aden International Airport.

The **Avianca S.A.** Colombian 747 (five -100s and two -200s) in orange livery also became an icon of the region. An ex-Continental -100 started the service in 1975, which Avianca would own outright as a first by a South American airline (significantly Pan Am had previously owned a stake in Avianca). The airline operated a very successful and financially viable service to New York, and from Bogota to Madrid, Paris and Frankfurt using its -100 and -200 fleets. A -200 Combi service offered great adaptability for commercial loads. Latterly two more -200s were leased in. Alongside KLM and Qantas, Avianca recently celebrated 100 years of service under its own name, but few commentators are aware of such history. All bar one of Avianca's fleet were second-hand airframes. Sadly, Avianca lost a -200B as Flight 011 on 27 November 1983 (HK2091OX Olafo) at Madrid due to controlled flight into terrain (CFIT): only 11 passengers survived and over 150 on board were killed.

VIASA of Venezuela claimed 747 operating bragging rights for its 747 service from 1971 – but as joint operations, these were wet-leased via its tie-up with a KLM service and

therefore not solely VIASA affairs. Cleverly, KLM supplied a 747 as the PH-BUG with the appropriate name *The Orinoco* on the nose (Venezuela's main river) for the VIASA wet-lease services to and from Europe. Interestingly, the VIASA /KLM service saw a mixed-sector VIASA/KLM flight and cabin crew roster with VIASA crews operating major portions of the routes. So many enthusiasts argue over which airline was South America's 747 pioneer operator.

VARIG do Brasil (of Brazil) operated four -200s (three ex-Air Hong Kong and one ex-SAA) from 1981 to 1986 and five -300/-300Cs (from ILFC, also ex-Atlas Air) from 1985 to 2000. A -400 operational history was of great note at VARIG from 1991, notably on Brazil–Europe services with three -400s (ex-ILFC) that also ranged as far as Japan, Hong Kong and Thailand, as well as a service to South Africa. Delivered 1991–3, the -400s were high-cost leases and this rare operation was terminated early in 1994.

LAN Chile operated an Irish-registered -100 ex-Aer Lingus (EI-BED) in full-LAN Chile livery for two years, 1988–90.

Air Pacific -400 DQ-FJQ (Fiji) heads home from Sydney with the gear just packed away. (Author)

Heavy and hot, Air Pacific makes a low-angle climb-out. The triple-slotted flaps are about to be raised a touch. (Author)

African 747s: African governments with airlines as instruments of prestige often secured a single or handful of 747 airframes. Well-known smaller African fleets included those of Royal Air Maroc, Air Algérie, Air Afrique, Air Gabon, Tunis Air and Cameroon Airlines. Egypt Air operated 747s including the -300. Arik Air of Nigeria cancelled its ambitious -800 order. Of note, Super VC10-operator East African Airways leased in an Aer Lingus -100 (EI-ASJ) on occasion. This airframe ended up at Kabo Air. South African Airways had a shiny fleet of 747s including the wonderful -SP.

Nigeria Airways, and Nigeria itself, have an interesting passenger and cargo 747 fleet history, to put it mildly. Numerous 747 airframes from major names have found their way to Lagos and Kano for reincarnation. Nigeria Airways leased in 747s and operated a code-share operation with Virgin which led to Virgin Nigeria Airways as a registered entity during 2004–10, but the 747 was not included in its fleet.

Previous Nigeria Airways liaisons with BOAC/BA, and then KLM management teams, saw a Nigeria Airways resurgence but the airline failed post-2000. The Nigeria Airways fleet included -100s, -200s, -200Ms, -200Fs and a rare -300 (Air Atlanta lease). An unusual Nigerian 747 was the ex-Korean Air -300SR with 550 seats all-economy, registered as 5N-DBK operated by **Max Air**.

Kabo Air had an ex-United, ex-Corsair -400 as late as 2020. Prior to that, it acquired 11 -100s and nine -200s from former mainline carriers. **Air Malawi** operated a (SAA) fully liveried -SP but this was a political status exercise and a short-lived lease. **Air Madagascar** flew a sole -200M from 1979 for several years. **Air Gabon** often flew its -200 into London Gatwick.

South African Airways (SAA) do of course have a 747 history of grander proportions, having operated 28 747s. SAA's first 747 in 1971 was registered ZS-SAN – the beloved -200B *Lebombo*, which plied the world's airways in style and safety, initially in a stunning colour scheme with a unique forward fuselage livery design. SAA operated a niche squadron of -SPs (running more than six, up to final service in 2003) and notably a world record flight from Seattle to Cape Town on 23 March 1976, a distance of 16,560 kilometres in just over 17 non-stop hours. A direct SAA Johannesburg–Sydney service via a polar great-circle routing was the -SP's territory. SAA operated ten -200s, including a -212F and originally flew three -300s. Post-Apartheid, SAA's -400s started arriving from 1991 with six passenger variants and two freighters.

747: Other Operators

Air Atlanta
Air France
Air Madagascar
Air New Zealand
Air Pacific
Air Siam
Alia/Royal Jordanian
Alitalia
Asiana
Cargolux
El Al
EVA
Garuda Indonesia
Highland Express
Iberia
Iran Air
Korean Air
Mahan Air
Malaysian Airlines
Mandarin Airlines
Martinair
Middle East Airlines
Olympic Airways
Orient Thai Airlines
Philippines Airlines
Saudia Arabian Airlines
Scandinavian
Syrian Arab Airlines
TAP
Thai Airways

Air Malawi leased a SAA 747-SP as ZS-SPB for not much more than thirty days to profile the Malawian state visit to Great Britain and Europe in April-May 1985. Therefore this photograph of the -SP in full Air Malawi livery at Heathrow is rare. Air Malawi previously operated a Vickets VC10! (Author)

Approaching the runway at BKK with the tarmac just visible, a Qantas co-pilot gets the -400 VH-OJM stabilized with a nudge of power at 160 knots and 700 feet on finals as the author observes from the centre seat (Photo Author)

Flying the 747

Despite its huge size and intimidating visual presence, the 747 was a pilot's joy; it handled and responded with great accuracy and rewarded a light touch. This was no flying boat or massive prop-liner of a behemoth that required hauling about from the control column. Despite its size, 747 responds directly to the controls.

The 747 flight deck is small. The tumblehome of the upper fuselage crown shaping means that the side walls and windows are inclined inwards as their upper sections angle inwards to the fuselage spine. This means that the pilot sits deep in, rather than on, the machine and is integrated into the command post function. All the control analogue dials are set out to ergonomic experience and principles. Everything falls readily to hand or eye. Perhaps only the spectre of aerodynamic noise as the airflow swishes up the aircraft's lobe and upper body shaping creating increased airflow volume, can be cited of any note. Analogue cockpit 747s are the real thing, but such are the airframe and powerplant improvements to the -400 and -800, that their glass electronic cockpits do not detract from real flying: they enhance it – so long as no computer complacency is allowed to creep in on the act of digital flying. Flying with the standby analogue dials only, and the electronic screens turned off, was a quality-training requirement at quality airlines.

On the old analogue 747, the flight engineer's panel to the right of the flight deck provided a significant systems' management function, bringing the total number of dials on the analogue flight deck to over five hundred. From here the flight engineer truly managed the mechanical function of the aircraft and could pour on the power when required.

On takeoff, 747 needed aligning correctly with the nose-gear steering wheel. This on-ground task was to prove quite difficult to learn. Sitting on the runway's end, with the double-checked configuration settings – slats, flaps, stabilizer trim, engine pressure ratios and reference speeds on the mark, runway emergency procedures agreed – you stand the throttles gently up to about 25 percent of their movement, wait for fuel and fan blades to flow and spool up, and then gently slide the four levers as far forward as your operations' data has deemed necessary. If the runway is short, or if the runway is long and the aircraft heavy, then push the levers to their wall and watch the speed build. If you are going to go but the speed is slow to build, assess what's up and add power, or stop if known parameters allow. Don't just sit there if it looks iffy: do something! Take a decision and stick to it.

When 'OK, go', 'Speed building', then 'Eighty knots' are called, it is on to V1, and shortly afterwards, just above 150 knots + (weight and other factors considered), a firm but short pull back on the column through about three inches will unstick the main wheels and rotate the machine off the ground without scraping that long tail. Extra care is required at this point with the longer -800 body. A rotation rate of two to three degrees per second is required to create a sub-10-degree rotation angle. Once off and clear, then you can pull back a bit further and get 13–15 degrees of climb on the dial. If you want, 17 degrees is available providing the parameters allow, which they rarely do. Very heavy takeoff weight and local weather conditions (winds) might indicate a flaps-20 (instead of flaps-10) takeoff and a 13-degree climb angle to V2 and height clearance parameters, especially with the earlier engines fitted.

The full takeoff run might last up to 40 seconds, and at hot and high airfields a brakes off to V2 takeoff cycle might last 55 seconds and use over 8,500 feet of runway depending on airport height, aircraft weights, local winds and temperatures. Using 10,000 feet of tarmac might cause a few concerns though.

Senior Qantas Captain Hughes has just inspected his steed at LHR prior to commanding the QF002 back home on its 12,000-mile sector: wonderful days. (Author)

-400 central command console in flight. The reserve analogue dials are a welcome offer. (Author)

Passing through 200 feet it is 'Positive climb, gear up please', and the 20 seconds of rumbling and buffeting begins as the undercarriage doors shuffle about to accept the gear trucks up into the body.

If an engine fails now, leave it, and do not shut it off until you have passed 400 feet, then action the emergency shutdown procedures and do it firm and fast – but only once two (or three) people have agreed the correct engine to close down.

Assuming all four engines are running happily, take in the sound, especially if they are Rolls-Royce RB211-524 G or H/T variants at full max power – as the sound is incredible in its combination of roar, bark and pulsating whine.

Passing through 1,000 feet, then above 1,500 feet and then 220 knots, the first flap/slat retraction takes place, then, as speed builds and the wing is safe, bring in the remaining slats. Cleaned up, the rate of climb increases, the throttles can be eased back a nudge to conserve engine life and avoid Exhaust Gas Temperature (EGT) rises. Keep an eye on the Engine Pressure Ratio (EPR).

A close eye is kept on the engine temps, vibration meters and fuel flow with the engines at maximum power for several minutes – possibly up to the time limit allowed. If the machine is at very high weight, this climb-out period is the critical phase.

Passing through 5,000 feet, a palpable change in the takeoff tension takes place and with a deft touch or two on the control column, and the throttles, the machine begins to really fly. Then if you must, engage autopilot, dial in the height required and 747 sails upwards to spend the next ten to 15 minutes achieving its initial clearance-to-cruise height prior to fuel burn-off, weight decrease and a stage climb up beyond 20,000 feet to 25,000 feet, then 30,000 feet and upwards on the airway.

Providing the long-haul cruise has been achieved and all fuel flow targets and range calculations met, and all-weather requirements incorporated, the tension goes away until the landing phase some hours later.

747 does not normally land with tension, unless there is a 25–35-knot crosswind and/or limited visibility near the runways. The thing to do is get the approach stabilized early, nail the height capture and descent rate data, leave slat and flap selection as long as possible to save fuel, then drop them out, add some power and scythe gently down the glide path on the classic 3-degree approach. Spoilers armed, cabin secure, 180 knots at flaps 20, then gear down about three miles out, come back to 160 knots. Take a late clearance repeated back to the tower; don't get low and slow. '100 above' might be called out, needing a small tweak, then keep the engines spooled up as the final 'flaps 25' or 'full-flaps 30' selection tracks out, and it is straight onto the runway coming through 150 knots. Vital to remember is that you are higher up than the main gear, and must flare as the computerized voice call-out counts off the last twenty of your height.

The ground-effect cushion under the wing should help as the big Boeing squelches down oh-so lightly onto the main gear. Ram the thrust reversers in quick if the runway is short or you have landed a touch long. No faffing about as you are gently easing the nose gear onto the tarmac: add braking action on the wheels, pull the reverse thrust off before 55 knots latest to avoid stalling a compressor, and careen down the runway to your turn-off – being sure to 'go in deep' so you do not cut across the grass with the main gear on the axis of your turn – that would be problematic.

Such is the ease of that wonderful, smooth 747 landing. Of course, if there is a crosswind, the 747 will suffer roll, and in severe winds, be slammed down, up and sideways. Catching it all with deftly applied ailerons, and rudder soon becomes a technique to be kept practised. And watch out for scraping an engine pod as you keep the into-wind wing low, or if the wind tips the downwind wing towards the tarmac – 747-400 and 747-800 being more difficult in terms of pod-strike risks in a heavy crosswind landing. Don't risk stressing the main gear by kicking off the crosswind-compensating yaw angle you have dialled in, too late.

Here lies the difficult bit: kick-off the approach yaw angle with opposite rudder just at the second you are about to touchdown, get the gear swivelling straight, but keep the into-wind wing held low, but avoid a pod strike by holding it too low or by failing to resist the tip if the gust puts the other wing over towards a pod strike on the other side.

Once learned and regularly practised, it's not as daunting as it sounds, but adding speed on the approach because you have to due to weather, or technical issues, might just require experience at real hand-eye-foot-brain flying rather than the computerized magenta line or 'cross hairs digital flying engendered in those too accustomed to an easy electronic life. Typing in the numbers and following the coloured line on the computer screen is not going to work in heavy rain, low visibility or a gusting 35-knot+ crosswind on a busy day at LHR, JFK, ORD, BKK, MEL or under the scud somewhere in Northern Europe. This is when experience and recent practice counts.

China Airlines Flight 605 from Taipei to Hong Kong on 4 November 1993 saw the 747-400 shoot off the end, vault the wall and flop into the harbour as the first hull loss of a -400.

747 really does fly like a dream, which given its size is a testament to its designers.

-400 throttle quadrant seen in flight as the electronic screens glow. Don't touch anything! (Author)

Follow the magenta line but retain the ability to fly by hand with basic dials and be in command of the computer, not the other way around, was a skill not to be underestimated. (Author)

The Rolls-Royces of BA's BOAC-liveried -400. Pure nostalgia. (BA)

Incidents and Questions

In 1977, Pan Am and KLM suffered the tragedy of two 747s colliding on a foggy runway at Tenerife: mass fatalities resulted. No one on board the KLM 747 survived its attempt to vault over the Pan Am 747 which was innocently traversing the runway under air-traffic-control instructions. Numerous factors lined up to create the situation where the KLM machine started its takeoff roll in unclear circumstances. The rest of the story is tragic history.

Japan Airlines lost a fully loaded -100 due to structural failure after inadequate repairs had been previously performed upon the airframe. A United 747, operating Flight UA 811, lost a forward cargo door and fuselage/cabin skin section in flight on 24 February 1989 and survived but with some passenger lost. Air India lost a 747 on a transatlantic service due to a bomb explosion although other theories existed among the investigators.

This late-1980s period was a tough time for the 747. The aircraft was under scrutiny by its operators and manufacturer, but no likely design flaw was found, nor known. However, some repairs to the Section 41 ovaloid-shaped forward fuselage parts emerged from the fleet-wide global focus.

Section 41 and the further aft Section 42 are where the two parts (as S41 and S42 of the 747's front fuselage) are first joined together. At the rear Section 42 joins the front or head of the 747 main fuselage at the wingpoint section. Fatigue cracks at Section 41, and Section 42, became known at inspection circa 10,000 hours of airframe use and Boeing latterly had to invoke a major repair schedule – as did all aircraft makers and airlines during the time of the ageing airliner.

The front of the 747 (the first massive, non-circular pressurized fuselage) had a tough job: it had to carry its structural loads, resist aerodynamic stresses, absorb repeated and daily nose-landing gear impact stresses up into the airframe and absorb daily use of the main cabin door (Door 1 Left) as well as the main forward cabin door (Door 1 Right). Sections 41/2 also saw the heavy use of the forward cargo door and constant floor, hull and keel loadings. Then came the unequal loadings of the pressurized cabin and its pressurization cycles upon the uniquely ovaloid-shaped fuselage and its ribs, frames and skins. Boeing had to put thousands of hours into solving these issues.

The circumstances of the fatal TWA 747 in-flight explosion off the East Coast of America after departure for Rome from New York remain controversial: chafed wiring and central fuel tank vapours have been cited as the explosive triggers to airframe break-up in flight, but some contest this theory and claim that the breakup of the aircraft appears to be different to that in subsequent primary interpretations – with Section 41 alone coming off first and not with Sections 41 and 42 coming off together as a result of a fuel tank failure.

One truth is obvious: the TWA -800 airframe was due to receive major Section 41 modification reinforcements and the parts had been ordered and the schedule for repairs had been set.

The final word must go to Boeing, for not only did it modify the older 747 airframes, it redesigned Section 41's key component and incorporated that design into production from 747 airframe line number 686. The intended service life of the 747 was 20 years or 60,000 hours; many flew long beyond both those targets to 100,000 hours (several over 120,000 hours) which rather proves that Boeing's original 747 Fatigue Integrity programme was accurate. But Section 41 did raise its head from seemingly unknown and unpredicted circumstances. We should, in fairness, note that the 747's official hull-loss and crash statistic per-million departures (flights) was lower than the industry average of large airliners and that several 747 hull losses were terrorist (not airframe) related.

747: The Closest Call?

One of the closest calls to disaster occurred on 1 February 1988 at London Gatwick when a Continental Airlines -100 suffered engine failure at a critical moment – on takeoff, just as the aircraft rotated off the runway.

The heavily laden aircraft – operating Flight CO 31 – struggled in severe crosswinds (and possible windshear) to fly level and to retain a climb rate; the stick-shaker activated. In fact, the 747 then came so close to hitting a nearby hillside that it reputedly left engine exhaust burn marks in the field. However, this was not evidenced in the consequent official report. The radio-altimeter reading is reputed to have gone below 50 feet, as some allege, possibly as low as 12 feet, but this remains anecdotal. A witness situated near the brow of the hill, 2,500 metres from the airport boundary, cited in the official AAIB report, stated that the aircraft 'just' cleared the roof of a farmhouse. However, the aircraft's DFDR flight recorder information cited a minimum height of 105 feet above ground level – which some may say was close enough.

Somehow, with the pilot adjusting the roll, yaw and the vital pitch control, and controlling the thrust asymmetry with major rudder and aileron inputs, and using the required maximum power at EPR 1.45 to the remaining three engines, the 747 remained flying. An extension to a briefly excessive climb angle of 22 degrees was likely to have resulted from the wind factors and aerodynamic forces upon the aircraft at a critical flight handling phase when the pilot was trying to save the aircraft and was corrected very quickly as the pilot assessed all that was happening and reacted amid multiple warnings and events. Of note, the aircraft was equipped with Pratt & Whitney JT9-A-specification engines of lower thrust rating (and with engine bleed valves off).

Having used right rudder on the takeoff roll to counteract the crosswind, the pilot then had to use a lot of opposing left rudder to control the asymmetric (outboard engine) thrust failure just as the aircraft took to the air in continuing cross, quartering wind forces. This would have placed major demands upon the aerodynamic performance of the aircraft and upon the handling pilot. With the flight engineer also beginning an immediate fuel dump, the 747 scraped along and very slowly clawed its way upwards and not further downwards.

Due to very high indicated engine exhaust gas EGT temperatures and the likelihood of a major fire, the flight engineer was forced to slightly reduce the No. 4 engine's thrust, doing so below 400 feet, thence to have to shut it down quickly. Evidence of a possible un-commanded thrust reduction in the No. 1 engine at rotation with witness-reported flames from it, was also cited as potentially circumstantial to the events, but unproven. The aircraft did not initially retain its climb profile and temporarily did not meet its three-engined performance expectations. Local weather conditions, notably that quartering wind, must have played a significant role.

We can observe that this 747 pilot and his crew had more than their hands full on a low-powered early 747 variant in one of the closest calls to major disaster the 747 has ever experienced.

The aircraft involved was in fact N605PE – the former People Express airline airframe. The No. 4 engine which failed at Gatwick had been rebuilt, but also had a recent previous history of a compressor stall during thrust reverse at Los Angeles, and an aborted takeoff at Honolulu, due to surging. No major faults were found and the engine remained in service but after the Gatwick incident, the No. 4 engine was found to have anomalies in its internal mechanisms (bleed RABS solenoid valves) and these may have been evidenced by the

two prior engine performance issues at Los Angeles and Honolulu prior to the Gatwick event. At Gatwick, a major leak in the No. 4 engine's high-pressure compressor section, and other engine component conditions, created the on-takeoff engine thrust failure. In this near-disaster, the 747 came through thanks to skilful flying by the pilot and the inherent nature of Sutter's amazing aircraft.

Every airliner suffers in-service incidents and events which seem abnormal to the non-aviation-experienced observer but which are routine to pilots and operators. 747 was designed to cope with such events and is loved by its pilots for just that ability.

On 29 December 2000 a mentally ill passenger gained access to the flight deck of BA's -400 G-BNLM, operating Flight BA2069 LHR-NBO. He attacked the flight crew and grabbed the controls and sent the aircraft into a stall warning and a series of very serious aerobatic-type flight manoeuvres as the crew and passengers fought to remove him. The first officer regained control and level flight was regained after a major height excursion. The airframe withstood the severe plus and minus g-forces imposed. All on board survived. Mr Boeing built the 747 strong.

Qantas was very fortunate not to suffer loss on 25 July 2008 when an oxygen

Above: Dream Lifter's hinged rear section was unique. (Boeing)

Left: 747 Dream Lifter with the highly unusual fuselage extension. (Boeing)

cylinder exploded on board the -400 VH-OJK during mid-cruise. The fuselage was torn open, ruptured at the wing root and depressurization occurred, but the 747 and the Qantas flight crew saved the day for an emergency landing with the aircraft's structure intact apart from a large hole in the forward cabin. The fail-safe design features and clever construction had worked.

Later 747 Airframe Issues
Perhaps the only really significant ongoing lifetime 747 mechanical issue across all variants is the complicated flaps and their systems. Remember, these are in full use on every flight in all conditions and are vital to the safe handling of the aircraft at lower speeds. The triple-slotted section flaps, with their massive sections run on tracks which feature canoe fairings: a complex series of mechanisms drive the flaps out to a 30-degree sweep and then return up into the wing and their storage voids. As with the Sutter-designed 727 wing, the 747's flaps and slats are supremely efficient in adding area and lift to the wing at low speeds.

The 747's flaps are huge dynamic forces, subject to weather, winds, buffet and of course, foreign-object damage thrown up from runways. Engine exhaust efflux flows through gaps in the flap sections and thrust dampers add roll control. But the flaps were to prove high maintenance items with regular need for metalwork, repairs and flap-track function attention. The risk of flaps on one side extending or retracting in an uneven or asymmetric setting was an issue to watch for, as was degradation to the metal edges of the flaps. A special watch had to be kept on the flap to rear-spar mountings too – keeping the bolts tight was vital.

Metal fatigue and delamination (in respective synthetic parts) of the wing trailing edge and flap systems became a maintenance item and monitoring of the 747's No. 4 flap track attachments was an inspection requirement. Minor flap problems in flight would be signalled by vibration, and in one famous incident, a large section of flap fell off an Indonesian -200 on approach to Gatwick Airport. A flap fracture could lead to the requirement for full aileron to regain control: as late as 1988 a British Airways -100 suffered such a flap fracture event.

Of note, the 747-SP replaced the triple-section flaps with simpler section flaps of lighter weight and easier actuation. Corrosion, skin repairs, patches and repairs to frames and stringers were all the stuff of normal airliner airframe life. The issue of engine-mounting fuse-pin design was raised by the El Al 747 cargo airframe crash at Amsterdam in 1992 and the prior China Airlines engine detachment incident of 29 December 1991. Replacing the main wing box parts and major floor beams was also required work on high-cycle airframes – unsurprisingly.

The 747 cargo door latch 'problem' also emerged as a design issue during the normal course of operational reporting in early service life and the manufacturer produced a Service Bulletin and a modification process. This was not an emergency Airworthiness Directive so did not require immediate works. The 1989 United Airlines 747 cargo-door incident airframe had not embodied this modification. A Pan Am 747 had previously suffered a similar unlatch after takeoff from London Heathrow but no accident ensued. Was it the door latching mechanism or the electrics that was the initial problem? It would be 1992 before the

The complicated 747 flap systems seen close up. Regular maintenance of the flap tracks and drives was essential. (Author)

NTSB took a further look at the issue and decided that an electrical wiring/circuit problem (rather than consequential metal locking mechanism design failure) was the principal probable cause.

Like any in-service airliner, 747 required regular scheduled maintenance and various rebuild and reinforcement measures – notably around the well-used main forward cabin door frame, and the rear main fuselage deck cargo door on Combi variants. A lifetime of loads and heavy landings might dimple the rear fuselage panels and this, allied to metal fatigue, would see heavy reinforcement plates added to the rear fuselage with extra riveting required.

2020: Last Landings

The withdrawal of mainline passenger 747s (principally the -400) began in 2016 and was hastened by the events of 2020. -400s were sent out to rest fallow at airports all over the world and the photographs final capture the mood of -400s awaiting their unknown fates. Sadly, not least for the BA fleet, the scrapman beckons with his scythe. In these photos we see the dismemberment of once-proud blue-riband 747s. It seems incredible, but it is true. Photographed at Cotswold (formerly Kemble) Airport with the assistance of Cotswold Airport and Air Salvage International.

Flaps and spoilers deployed at full angles. (Author)

Corsair's ex-UAL -400s prior to scrapping or conversion to cargo status after their end of passenger service. Corsair also operated a single -SP. (Author)

Engine details with an empty casing and others framing their rest at Cotswold Airport's 747 graveyard. (Author)

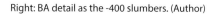

Above: Flying the flag from the -400 flightdeck escape hatch as BA ends its five-decades of 747 operational history on 8 October 2020 in a rural field at Cotswold Airport. (Author)

Right: BA detail as the -400 slumbers. (Author)

Above: The final landing. BA's G-CIVB sinks into Cotswold Airport as the last ever BA 747-400 flight. With a strong headwind on finals, the lightly laden aircraft's landing air-speed was at sub-140 knots, very low indeed, and its ground-speed even lower. (Author)

Right: BA's -400 with One World titles and two engines removed at the end of its life. (Author)

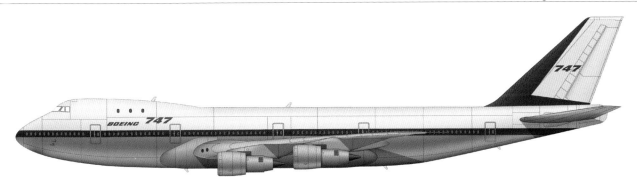

Boeing's 747 original flight-test prototype machine number one in the then Boeing house livery. This machine (RA001) as N7470 was latterly defined as a reverse-engineered -100 from which the first 747 customer number of Pan Am's -121 iteration became production airframe reality. The machine illustrated was first rolled out on 30 September 1968 and first flown on 9 February 1969 and was subjected to an extensive flight-test programme, carrying many tons of testing equipment. Service entry would of course be delayed by the problems with the Pratt & Whitney JT9D-3A engines. Used for flight-testing across all the 747 engine upgrades and Pratt & Whitney, General Electric and Rolls-Royce powerplants, the aircraft would be preserved at Seattle but then re-enter test-flying for the Boeing 777's engine programme.

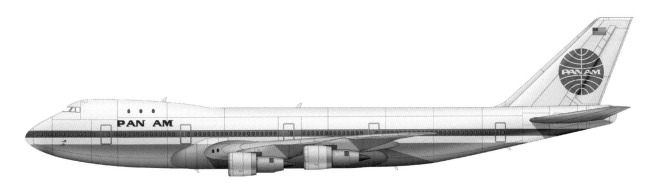

The Pan American World Airways (Pan Am/PA) 747s were early enough not to have the -100 Boeing nametag, so initially were -21s (as per Pan Am's Boeing customer code), only then to become -121s. The Pan Am airframes operated in a series of defined liveries and several hybrid schemes. They all had names prefaced by the old Clipper titles from the Pan American Airways Clipper flying boat days. Pan Am operated 44 -100s, 10 examples of the -200s and the wonderful sight of 11 -SPs. 747 Constructor/Construction Number 19639, as Line Number 2 as N747PA was first into service in 1969 and a great deal of work was required to achieve reliable dispatch and sector schedules. Eventually, the Pan Am 747s, notably the -100-series airframes, often topped 80,000 flying hours on the airframe – with some exceeding 85,000 hours – way beyond Boeing's intended design life amid takeoff and landing and pressurization cycles (often over 20,000) in the airframe total hours. One Pan Am -100 exceeded 90,000 hours up to Pan Am's collapse, but even that figure would be exceeded by TWA's -100s. Several veteran classic 747s achieved figures exceeding 115,000 hours and 35,000 cycles. The livery depicted – with three upper-deck windows extant, shows the -100 as a true Pan Am classic.

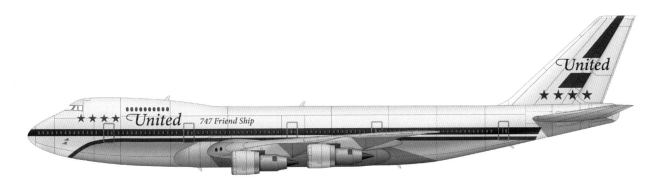

United Airlines showing the truly classic 1970s 747 livery taken from the United DC-8s, this is the Friendship scheme as applied to United's early batch of 747s, the first of which was Constructor Number 19753 N4703UA first flown in April 1970 as a -122 variant. United took 18 -122s and then a second delivery of two -222s with the more powerful engines, longer range and higher takeoff weights, in 1987. It would be years before its next 747s arrived. A series of livery updates would result. *Friendship One* was the United 747-SP that set a speed record for flying around the world in 36 hours, 54 minutes and 15 seconds. United nearly lost a 747 over the Pacific in February 1989 when N4713UA hit trouble in the famous cargo-door incident, but great flying saved the day. The cargo-door mechanism, not the airline, was deemed at fault. The UA fleet included nine -100s with five -100SFs. The -200 fleet totalled ten -200-series with four -200Bs, three -SPs, one -200SF and one -200BSF. The United -400 fleet topped 16 -400s, one of which, N106UA, latterly found its curious way to Blue Sky Airlines and saw later use by Mahan Air Iran before being sold on to Phuket Airlines. United's liveries evolved into differing themes and its 1990s scheme was very similar to the British Airways Landor livery.

Trans World Airlines' new -100s carried its Boeing customer number of 31, as -131, but one of its 747s (Reg N307TW) was a -38 – which meant it came from customer -38: the Qantas customer code. Two TWA -100s were -136s, meaning that they were ex-British Airways. Curiously, several ex-TWA airframes ended up in service in Iran and flew on for years in varying states of repair. The depicted livery is the later revised scheme that updated the 1960s Star Stream livery as seen on 707s and early TWA 747s. TWA's first 747 delivery was on 31 December 1969 with Constructor Number 19667. Twelve -131s were originally ordered, followed by four more. The TWA -SPs arrived in 1979.

Northwest (Orient) was a transpacific and US domestic operator. Northwest Orient operated a superb niche 747 operation and was an early recipient with the first -100 as a -151 with Constructor Number 19778 arriving first as a programme of deliveries in the summer and autumn of 1970 for service entry from late that year onwards. Nine more -151s were delivered. NWO took 25 -200s, of which 16 were its own -251 customer variants. New colours and revised engines were retrofitted to the fleet that soon also ranged across the Atlantic. Northwest took more -200s and scooped up cancelled orders from ex-Iranian and ex-Braniff orders. Northwest also made cargo tracks with eight -251Fs, one 2J9F, and added passenger capacity with two -227Bs. The red-tailed NOW machines were a fine sight and proudly operated.

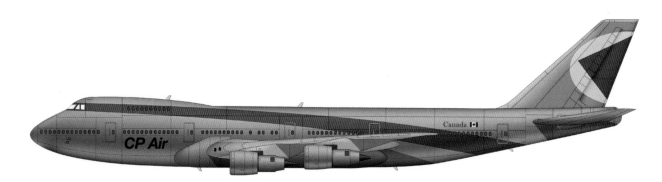

Canadian Pacific – CP Air – used orange style long before Braniff used the hue too. Rooted in early Canadian railway history, Canadian Pacific was truly historic and ordered four -217s in 1973, having previously been a DC-8 devotee. Transpacific and transpolar routes to Europe were first served in 1973 with the orange-topped, polished metal bodies providing a quintessential Canadian service out of its Vancouver base. -200B Constructor Number 20801 as C-FCRA arrived at the end of 1973 for crew training and subsequent service entry. C-FCRB flew in from Paine Field on new delivery two weeks later. The airline took to the DC-10 trijet and its 747 operations were, despite daily services to major European cities, set to recede. Pakistan Airlines snapped up C-FCRA and three sister airframes. The great Canadian airline itself disappeared in a corporate shuffling of Canadian air transport in 1987, to emerge as Canadian Airlines International.

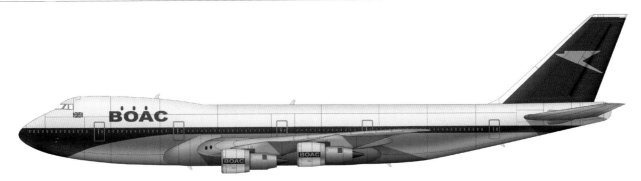

The British Overseas Airways Corporation (BOAC) merged with British European Airways (BEA) to form the new British Airways (BA) in 1974, but from April 1970 BOAC became the owner of a 747-100 or -136 with Constructor Number 19761 as G-AWNA. Painted up in the stunning elegance of BOAC blue, with a golden Speedbird on the fin, this was the first of BOAC's batch of over a dozen JT9D-powered -100s. She and some of her sister ships would serve BOAC and then BA right up to the Landor livery era of the 1990s.

Post-1974 BOAC saw 747 upgrades such as upper-deck window conversions, more power and better avionics on the original -136 fleet. BA took more examples of the developing -136 to a fleet total of eighteen. Then came 14 -236Bs, five bought-in -200 Combis and a briefly deployed Freighter. By early 1977 BA was fitting Rolls-Royce RB211-524 D4 engines to its -236 fleet, but the remaining old BOAC -136 original G-AWNA to G-AWNP-coded airframes staggered on with Pratt power, which provided some interesting hot-and-high takeoff moments in the tropics. The Negus-designed livery is depicted here with the word airways, minus its capital letter as designed. Pre-BA privatization, this was BA's global image and it needed an urgent update for a new era.

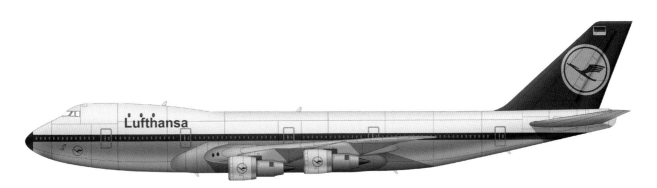

Lufthansa was the first non-American airline to grab a new 747 airframe off Boeing with Constructor Number 19746 D-ABYA as a -130 first flying in February 1970, and in March soon finding its way from Paine Field to Frankfurt Main. D-ABYB would follow on a few weeks later. Lufthansa had two shiny new 747s before any other European airline. (Alitalia, Air France and BOAC would soon catch up). Lufthansa's third -120 would follow in months and its first -230B would arrive a year later. Lufthansa would take over 30 Classic 747 variants across -130 to -230B. The -230F D-ABYE was the first-ever windowless 747, as a nose-loading Freighter without main cabin windows. The more powerful General Electric engines and the -200B and -200B Combi specifications became Lufthansa default choice across the 1980s.The airline shared its 747s with its Condor sub-brand, with the only thing changed on the livery being the name.

Koninklijke Luchtvaart Maatschappij means Royal Dutch Airlines – better known as KLM. But it waited for the -200B, so its first tranche of aircraft began with Constructor Number 19922 first flying on 13 December 1970 as the -206B PH-BUA *The Mississippi*, which featured the earlier white tail and white-top livery prior to the new KLM blue top and revised tail livery of 1972 onwards. KLM took seven early 200Bs (losing one at Tenerife) with Pratt & Whitney powerplants. Then the General Electric CF6 engines were specified with the first arriving in 1975 as PH-BUH, and it was these GE-powered -206s that were latterly very interestingly converted to KLM's SUD long-top upper deck based on an original short-top airframe. Nine 206B Combis were ordered and subsequently converted to SUD status. The true EUD -300-series arrived as -306 and -306M airframes from 1983 onwards. These classic 747s were also treated to an electronic flight instrumentation system upgrade from their analogue flight decks. KLM's blue was latterly slightly revised but remains the ultimate livery design classic.

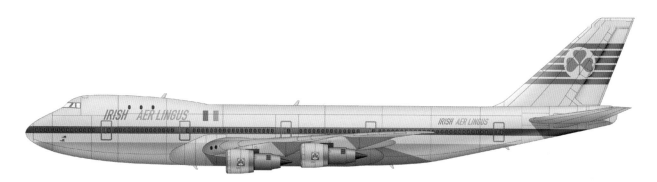

Aer Lingus: Irish International was a keen Boeing 707 operator and an early 747 buyer on a small scale and became a highly respected 747 operator and maintenance outfit that leased out spare 747s to premier world carriers when required. This original livery profile predated the green-top scheme that seemed similar to KLM's blue-top design in all but hue. Aer Lingus took its first -100 as Constructor Number 19745 EI-ASI in November 1970 as a -148, and another arrived by March 1971. Aer Lingus had to lease in a third 747 when it got caught out needing extra capacity when one of its own airframes was out on lease to another carrier. The Irish 747s were perfectly maintained, luxurious, had superb cabin service and experienced flight crews, carving a very characterful niche – perhaps in some ways doing for Irish 747 operations what Ward Air did for Canadian 747 operations.

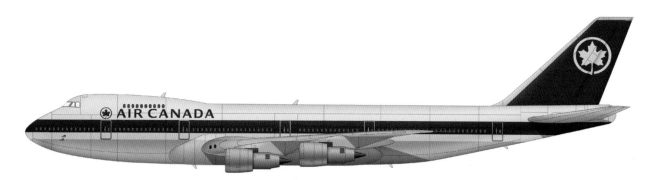

Air Canada's -133 Constructor Number 20013 CF-TOA first flew in January 1971 (serving the airline for nearly 12 years), and CF-TOB arrived two months later, from Montreal Dorval and from Toronto Lester B. Pearson operational bases respectively. Air Canada (AC) services began in April 1971, initially providing a transcontinental domestic 747 service and then to overseas sectors. By 1975 the fifth of Air Canada's -133s had been delivered. Air Canada also received three 200s, the first being C-GAGA, and it took the first full-production -200 Combi 747 original (non-modified) airframe in 1975. One -200 came in from Qantas. A gap occurred prior to -400 deliveries, commencing in 1991. Several ex-Canadian Airlines International airframes joined the AC fleet. A final all-white livery with a revised tailfin marked the last years of the 747s at Air Canada. The livery depicted here is the earlier scheme yet the variation that removed the original large black glare shield treatment to the nose. The Maple Leaf branding on the fin was very noticeable and popular. Air Canada's 747s were a vital national tool and symbol prior to the type's last flight with AC on 31 October 2004, closing 33 years of service.

Queensland and Northern Territories Aerial Services – Qantas – waited for the -200B and took its first as Constructor Number in July 1971. Within seven years it had amassed a superbly maintained fleet of nearly 20 long-haul 747 airframes, which included one Combi variant. The first Qantas machines had the rare lower-deck galley and the early conversion of the upper-deck lounge to standardized all-passenger seating with more windows. The early fleet were Pratt & Whitney-powered but Qantas became an all-747 and all-Rolls-Royce 747 operator from late 1979. Here we see the shortbodied -SP in classic Qantas ochre livery prior to the new scheme of the late 1980s. Note the shorter body and taller tailfin. The -SP variant now has a major enthusiast following. Also shown is one of six -338s that Qantas operated prior to the introduction of the -400. Constructor Number 23222 VH-EBT arrived in October 1984 and Concorde test pilot, E. Brian Trubshaw himself, was much amused. The Qantas long-haul network aided the -300's marginal economy improvements and Qantas made the most of an EUD Business Class upstairs. Ultra-reliable and Rolls-Royce-powered, -300 was popular at Qantas (as it was at SAA and KLM) but the -400 was soon to arrive.

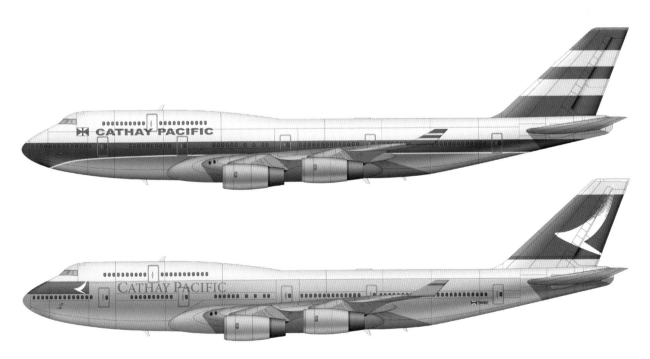

Hong Kong-based Cathay Pacific Airways (Swire Group) with call-sign CX truly was a pre-1997 Hong Kong legend and yet came late to the 747. Its first 747s were Rolls-Royce-powered -200Bs of 1979 delivery and optimized for ultra-long-haul and transpacific sectors. Constructor Number 21746, appropriately registered VR-HKG, began a stream of -267B airframe-coded deliveries for the dawn of the 1980s and Cathay's new era. By 1985, eight -267Bs formed a core CX-coded operation out of Hong Kong Kai Tak. Next up came six -367s which by late 1999 were moved on via lease to PIA. Then arrived the -400 as the -467 in the classic CX old green-striped livery seen here. Seeing one of these do a 47-degree turn into Kai Tak in the rain was truly awe inspiring. Also shown is the -467 in the revised and rather bland post-2000 livery design that stayed with the fleet until its demise.

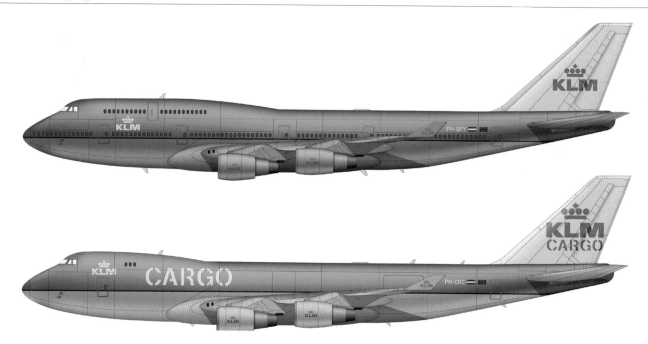

KLM saw its -200s and -300s, and their interesting history, move on to the -400 when the airline took early options on the wingletted wonder. KLM made full use of the Combi concept with its -406-series machines. Five -400s arrived from 1989 and 17 of the versatile Combi -406Ms followed. Also shown is PH-CKC, of note, the -406F/ER cargo machines had the nose door and the SCD – the large rear side door – with the short-top upper deck and special KLM CARGO titling. Three -406Fs were operated via the Martinair link-up with varying liveries. In total, from -206 to -406, KLM has operated nearly 40 747s.

United's -400 as -422-coded N106UA joined the fleet in June 1994 with over 40 to follow. The fleet wore various liveries. Many think that the golden globe tail design and the blue design with blue engines and lower body were the best. An earlier grey-topped livery, akin to the 1990s BA scheme, was somewhat dull and derivative. Latterly amalgamated with Continental, United operated its last -400 service on 19 October 2017, ending 47 years of 747 flying at UAL. Of note, several ex-United -422 airframes were key members of the Corsair all-economy seating fleet with over 560 seats on certain configurations.

Northwest and NWA: after its -100 and -200 years, the newly named Northwest followed up with 16 -400s, with the last delivered in May 2002. NW took the development -400 airframe N401PW, which then became N661US, as the -400 launch machine as a NW -451-coded airframe but vied with Singapore Airlines' -400 for international debut honours. This airframe was then to see later Delta Airways service. The revised NW livery retained the historic red top and served on a code-share tie-up with KLM Royal Dutch Airlines to and from Amsterdam's European hub. Transpacific sectors remained a core NW operational theme up to withdrawal in 2016. Of note, a later white-bodied livery with a red tail was seen on the -451s with NWA titles as late as 2010, prior to the demise of NWA, but here we stick with the earlier Northwest-style livery tradition in its last incarnation. Delta refurbished much of the fleet and the rest of the NW 747 story is operational history.

The British Airways Landor agency-designed livery was from early 1984, to replace the earlier Negus livery and took BA into a new privatized era of smart service with a red speedline aping the speedwing out of the original Speedbird design, as seen here on a BA -436. The traditional white-top fuselage was replaced with a corporate-themed grey hue. The quartered Union Jack flag design was retained on the tail. By 1999 the newer Chatham livery and the various tailfin designs had emerged. Two distinct batches of BA -436s were registered from first delivery in 1989 to last arrival in 1999 as at BA (G-B … and G-C …). The last BA -436s were prematurely retired in 2020 but not before three nostalgic retro liveries had been applied to three of the airframes.

Lufthansa's fading colours: depicted here we see the -430 with the traditional Lufthansa tailfin livery with a yellow circle and a blue flying bird in a blue fin. However, the blue full-length cheatline has gone and we see a typical all-white fuselage design treatment of the era. The Lufthansa -430 fleet served as premier route flagships prior to the arrival of the Airbus A380 fleet at the airline. Yet Lufthansa's crews and passengers adored the -430 fleet – which were maintained and operated to the very highest standards. First Class was upstairs in an exclusive zone but, on later -430s and the new -830I fleet, Business Class was situated in the long-top cabin instead. When the -800I as -830I arrived, Lufthansa launched its new colour scheme to much criticism. Gone was the yellow-circled tail and the traditional dark blue. So dark was the new blue seen on the tail that it had to be revised to a brighter shade to avoid appearing black. The all-white fuselage and engines took even more cleaning time and costs. The -830I fleet also reactivated Lufthansa's original 1970s 747 registrations.

Boeing launched the 2015 -800I range in a red version of its spectacular new corporate airframe livery first seen in blue. Here we see the red/orange version applied to the test airframe -800I. Note the longer fuselage, longer upper deck and completely revised wing and shorter/higher angled engine pylon mounting to accommodate the larger Gen Ex engines. Of interest, the -800F re-employs the long-abandoned short-top upper-deck lobe to reduce weight and remove unwanted passenger capacity. The -800 series may add at least another 25 years to the 747's 50-year service. 747 as an airframe may achieve 75 years' service, which would be true testament to its genius.

Modelling the 747

KLM's wonderful and timeless livery captured in diecast brilliance as the 747-200 variant. The Aviation Retail Direct ARD200 reflects its high-quality origins amid the diecast 747 movement and its massive market. Inflight 200 were the original 1/200-scale diecast suppliers, then Herpa moved from 1/200 plastic construction to metal, and now Aeroclassics, ALB, Big Bird, Blue Box, Dragon Wings, GeminiJets, Hobby Master, JC Wings, Jet X, NG, Owl Wings, Phoenix, Retro, Seattle Models and Western Models, all supply 1/200 airliner models in a wonderful 747 diecast world. Hogan, Skymarks, and Flight Miniatures also supply 'snap-together' 1/200 747 models at a lower cost sector. Boeing themselves have purchased an Inflight 200 1/200-scale model of the original -100, so that tells the reader just how well regarded the diecast 747 story has become.

Modelling the 747 has occupied the minds of many enthusiasts over the years. With the many variations and sub-sets to the 747, a superb array of technical specifications provides focus for the modeller – as does the long history of many wonderful, and occasionally weird, livery designs. 747 modelling is huge the world over, proving how much the 747 is loved.

Initially a plastic/resin/injection/vac-form moulded kit, the 747 model range from **Airfix**, **Revell** and **Heller** set the kit scene from the 1970s onwards. This has evolved over five decades into a wider range of kits and into synthetic, diecast, wood, GRP, foam and other materials for 747 modelling Radio-control 747 models with ducted fan engines have also been constructed in a hybrid blend of materials: lightweight GRP and plastic offer great efficiencies for the radio-control, large-scale modeller. Today, the market focus is on diecast 747s, which are being issued at a rate that really has created a new niche.

747 models have predominately come in airline transport guise, but military variants from Air Force One and beyond have also become part of the scene. The current large-scale diecast movement that exists around the 747 market is booming with new releases being a key feature of 2020/1. The *Diecast Flier* proves the point about the diecast enthusiasm as do the

Airliner Café and *Model Airliner* websites which also provide excellent and valuable resources to the expert model airliner enthusiast – both covering many aspects of kit and diecast modelling. *Airliner-Civil-Aircraft-Modeller.com*, *AirNet*, *AeroModeller* and *Unofficial Airfix Forum* all provide online content and guidance on the finer points of airliner modelling.

The late Jon Proctor (who was the son of an American Airlines pilot and brother of a TWA pilot) was a writer, author, photographer, modeller and a leading guide to airliner details (not least via *Airliners* magazine) and its modelling. Many enthusiasts relied upon his knowledge and tutelage in the world of airliner and air transport enthusiasm. No coverage of airliner modelling or the 747 can go without tribute to one of the subject's leading lights.

For the static scale-model builder, 747 models came in scales of 1/72, 1/125, 1/144 and 1/200. Diecast offerings at 1/200 and 1/450 and 1/500 have been a more recent market. Inflight 200, Aviation Retail Direct, GeminiJets and JC Wings have all released 1/200 diecast ranges of 747s in dozens of liveries.

Preformed plastic airline models, such as those of **Wooster**, were at 1/250 scale. These may have been a bit basic in detail terms, but they offered easy access at a reasonable price.

Welsh Models, have produced an interesting niche range of 747 renditions using white metal and resin-cast hybrid construction.

The larger-scale diecast, resin-moulded and wooden models have become popular beyond the expert total-build scale-model market. Diecast lead manufacturers such as Inflight 200, Aviation Retail Direct, Aeroclassics, GeminiJets and Herpa Hogan now produce massive ranges of 747 types and liveries. Sky Classics, SkyMarks, Retro and JC Wings have turned out recent mouldings for the iconic 747.

Aviation Retail Direct (ARD), principally located near London Heathrow Airport, have a long history of service to aviation and airliner models and modelling, all under its well-known proprietor Paul Burge. ARD have an amazing global hub of a collectors' showroom of diecast and other types of 747 models (as well as a further Heathrow Airport shop) and can only be complemented on their achievement as a model emporium and 747 haven of worldwide fame. ARD have launched their own ARD 200 diecast range via a collaboration with the esteemed Inflight 200 brand. ARD have also obtained licences from airlines to reproduce livery and branded content for the expert modeller and enthusiast.

It could be argued that Inflight 200's diecast 1/200-scale 747 range, notably its -SP collection (in the entire repertoire of original AA, Qantas, Pan Am, United, SAA and other operator liveries), is currently regarded by some model enthusiasts as a truly significant collectors' item archive and an amazing 747 tribute. In 2021, Inflight 200's Qantas 747 tribute releases will become instant collectors' items. For balance, we should note that GeminiJets also produce 1/200-scale 747s of importance. JC Wings and Herpa both offer 1/200 747s gems too.

Our showcase model depicts the original of three generations of KLM's famous 747s and then expands it with their subsequent colours as diecast models and evidences the intricacies and superb effects now possible in structural and livery decal standards.

Up close and detailed, the windows, nose gear and polished-metal lower fuselage all reflect expert detailing and reproduction of the real thing.

KLM CLASSICS: A TRIO OF DIECAST DELIGHTS

KLM 747-206B, PH-BUB 1971 Early White-top Livery 1/200 by Inflight 200 Models

Diecast moulds for larger-scale models can cost many thousands of pounds, so the investment is serious and requires a high-quality result to justify the purchase price of a respective model. Licences from original airframe manufacturers and airlines all require negotiating. Inflight 200 are top-quality producers and each diecast model is hand built. The use of rotating engine fans, rolling tyres and, on some models, moveable items, add to this maker's class. However, to show the breadth and quality of the diecast marketplace we focus on this KLM classic white-top 1970s original-livery -200 depicting the 747 named *Nile* (*Nijl*) a superb rendition by Inflight 200 of this much-loved airline and its early 747.

Note the Pratt & Whitney JT9D engines' good detailing and accurate fuselage contours. Windows, titles and antenna all are well represented. Here is a little bit of classic KLM history captured as a model with real feeling and enthusiast appeal. Lamp/lighting rendition is excellent. Inflight 200 make models for airlines and authorities, not just collectors, and the high level of accuracy achieved can be seen in the accompanying shots. These models are not cheap, but they are top-class collectors' items and dedicated enthusiasts love them for their consistency, scaling, detail and accuracy. This one is so good that you can almost hear it spooling up on its stand.

Inflight 200 excelled with this KLM -200 in the earlier KLM white-top livery (also known as the KLM white-tail because the airline's tails had previously been blue-striped) prior to the 1970s with the now-famous KLM 'blue-top scheme'. The contours of the difficult-to-mould fuselage and its upper lobe have been superbly captured. With accurate printing, detailed engine fan blades and a turning nose wheel, allied to stunning build quality, you can almost hear those Pratt & Whitneys churning.

Details such as engine pylons, wing root and dihedral, are all framed by this utterly classic 1/200 model depicting the -200 named the *Nile* (*Nijl*). Inflight 200's early diecast models at 1/200 stunned the market with their quality, and only Herpa's (plastic 1/200) offered something at the same scale but at different build quality.

Comparing old blue and new blue, the -200 and the -400 releases seen tail to tail.

Few other diecast models get to this level of accuracy when it comes to engine casing and pylon design.

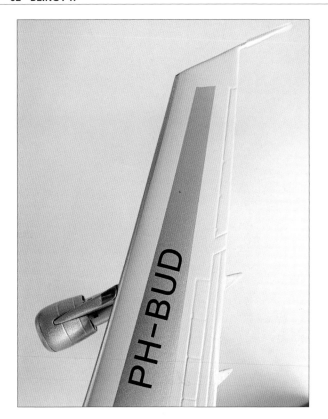

Note the very accurate upper-wing surface rendition in the correct paint and metal detailing of the PH-BUD; the wing strakes/fuel dump rods have been protected by their sheaths in this view. The model is over a foot long and has a wingspan that really makes an impression on a stand.

One of the common failings of 747 models is the thickness and moulding of the tailfin. Inflight 200 have got this one spot on. The variable incidence horizontal stabilizer or tailplane, is also very accurate.

Lobe, upper deck, lights and contours, it's all here. Note the original early -200 upper-deck three-window configuration – latterly modified in the real aircraft.

Down at the wing root is where even some expensive 747 models fail – even at 1/200, but this one gets it right.

Underbody scene gives you all you can get at 1/200. Wheels, tyres and beams are all close to reality in scaling and moulding.

Seen from above, the scale, sweep and stance of this model take it as close to the real thing as you can get in diecast. The KLM is perfectly rendered.

KLM 747-206B, PH-BUB Post-1972 Blue-top Livery, 1/200 by Aviation Retail Direct ARD200

In order to modernize its image, KLM rebranded in the early 1970s and came up with an amazing blue hue and branding logo that has endured timelessly across four decades. Woe betide the corporate suit that removes KLM blue!

This diecast 1/200 ARD200-branded model stems from the Aviation Retail Direct release (via a collaboration with Inflight 200) and depicts the KLM -206 PH-BUB *Danube* (*Donau*) as KLM's second -206B repainted in the famous blue branding livery. The colour is KLM blue – as vivid cerulean which moved KLM blue on from its original hue of dark blue, royal blue and gold highlights with a white-top fuselage and fin. Modellers should note that KLM blue is not the same colour as the paler Korean Air blue. KLM blue is closer to Bugatti blue that dates from the late 1920s.

In this superb model, every aspect of the classic KLM is captured and the scaling of the wing skin detailing, paint surfacing, static/fuel dump strakes and the shape of the fuselage are all spot on. HF/antenna, strobe and undercarriage details are also top quality – as they would be, given their tooling origins.

Produced in metal with some plastic detailing, as a 1/200 model with over 13 inches of body length and corresponding wingspan, the model can be displayed with a stand or on its expertly detailed undercarriage. The polished metal finish of the lower body is of particular excellence. The titles and scaling of livery details are all accurate. At over £100/$125 (new), this is not cheap, and not intended to be anything other than a quality item for the dedicated 747 enthusiast. The author purchased his KLM 747 ARD200 model at full price and, having worked on KLM 747s, knows that it is an accurate collectors' item.

Into the blue: KLM's revised blue-top livery of 1972 onwards was slowly applied to its original badge of white-top 747-200s. These were repainted during scheduled heavy maintenance. KLM's DC-10s were delivered from new in the blue-top scheme.

The new livery also changed the cheatlines – as the paint along the window line: from a royal blue window cheatline with pale blue line above, to a thicker royal blue window line with a thicker white line below. Note the superb accuracy of the ARD200 body and wing work – reflecting the Inflight 200 origins.

Seen on its stand at climb angle, only the lack of deployed slats and flaps gives the game away. But there are 747 models on the market at 1/200 scale with slats and flaps set in the deployed/out configuration.

Here the cargo door detailing is well shown; note also the main cabin-door hinge details. Even the tyres treads are accurate.

Under the wing we see the excellent engine, pylons, flaps, canoe-fairings and wing-skin details that mark out a truly high-quality diecasting. This is the standard that expert modellers and diecast fans have come to expect at the top of the market.

KLM white-top -200 and KLM blue-top -400 seen in diecast-quality company.

KLM 747-406 Blue Livery, 1/200 by Inflight 200 Models

What better way to celebrate diecast brilliance than by following up the KLM classics with Inflight 200's rendition of the -400 in later KLM blue – the revision in blue shade to the defining and iconic livery that reflected all of KLM's brand values and history: a slightly stronger or darker blue, with revised design treatment. Inflight 200 seek collectors' opinions on preproduction liveries so that the collector community can advise on accuracy. There is no doubt that Inflight 200's moulds and detailing quality have found a dedicated audience in the collector and av geek community. This model reflects the revised KLM blue, but not the KLM 100 anniversary lettering that closed the 747 story at KLM.

This model depicts the post-KLM–Air France merger and modifications to the famous early KLM blue livery seen on a -400, and includes the curved downsweep to the nose section of the main body colour and cheatlines. This revised frontal design modernized the KLM livery without losing the essential authenticity of KLM's blue legend, which became the massive marketing signature and brand hallmark for the airline – as well as being a stunning piece of industrial design.

The details from flaps to door surrounds, titles, engine scaling, pylons, fan blades and undercarriage all show how well Inflight 200 can do with its diecast tributes to airliner heritage. The only area some might query would be the underbody wing area detailing, but this would be nit-picking.

Here the elongated EUD upper deck of the -400 is captured. Note the later-style engine casings and pylons, all well rendered by Inflight 200's -400 model – complete with its winglets.

Both the -200 and the -400 tail details are correct. Note the auxiliary power unit (APU) exhaust detailing.

Above: Getting the fuselage contours correct is key, as is achieving the -400's revised wing-root fairing, both well detailed here.

Centre: Sleek, stylish and KLM blue, some will argue that it does not get any better. Note navigation/ landing lights set into the wing's leading edge. The top of the fuselage lobe crown is also perfect – unlike some other makes.

Bottom: Perfection of scale, detail and form are not easy to achieve. The fin-section thickness and rudder parts are crucial. The Inflight 200 casting has hit the mark here.

United Airlines Boeing 747-400 N104 UA Blue Tulip Livery, 1/200 by JC Wings

This is one of JC Wings' best and is notable for being the deployed flaps and slats version. The accuracy of this specific United livery paint codes (Rising Blue or Blue Tulip scheme) being spot on. JC Wings have turned out a good-quality casting with this model and apart from some minor lost points over the undercarriage detailing, and the possibly slightly thick engine pylons, the model presents as well scaled and superbly detailed. Pylons, panels and transitions are all good. The landing light jewels look real too. It really flies and captures the -400 design. Of note is the difficult-to-mould extended upper-deck shaping which is very accurate. If only the angle of the model's incidence upon its stand could be better modified to personal taste by the individual. A secure, multi-position, multi-axis lockable stand option has yet to appear in the design of model stands.

United's very complex tail livery was well captured in the printing and application to this model. The rudders are also clearly rendered.

This JC Wings' casting has got the fin and rear fuselage scaling and contours correct, although the rudder sections might lack definition.

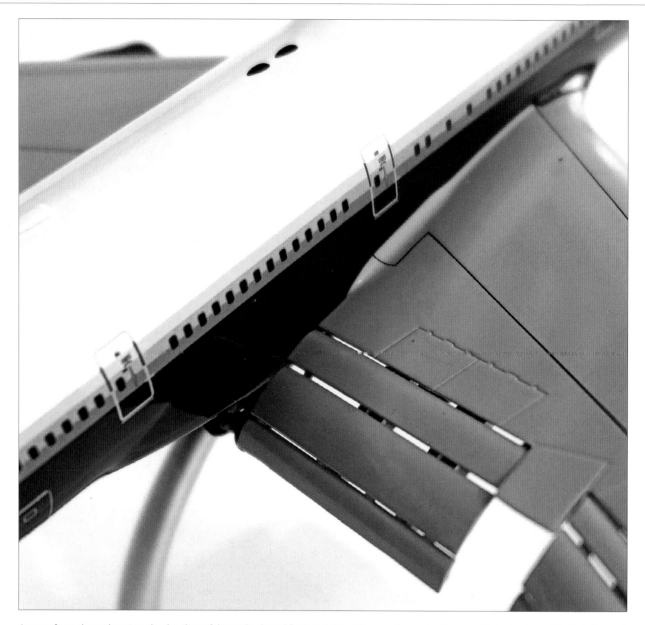

As seen from above the wing, the detailing of the triple-slotted flaps as deployed, correctly models the complicated nature of their design and operation.

Seen from underneath, the flaps mechanism and canoe-fairings are all well captured. Only the wing skin and pylons offer slightly less detail than the forensically minded might desire.

A brilliant capture of the leading-edge in-board Krueger flap/slat deployment setting added to the model's finesse.

The -400 upper-deck details and United's livery design are perfect – right down to the antennae.

-SP Specials

The shorter 747, the -SP, has a special following in the diecast and kit movement. Recently a vast range of liveries and decals has become available via many issues from leading manufacturers. Here we see Inflight 200's South African Airways -SP and a Middle Eastern VIP flight livery. Also shown is the Herpa 1/500 -SP in Air Nambia colours.

Smaller-scale diecast models at 1/400 and 1/500, have stemmed from the likes of Herpa, Hogan, GeminiJets and Big Bird. These have been well detailed as far as the scale allows, but are perhaps less finessed in details such as undercarriages, engines and structural aspects, yet they have provided the collector with strong renditions of liveries and types at more accessible prices.

The Big Bird-branded 1/500 models have existed through several ownerships of their moulds and licences and most enthusiasts feel that the detailing of these models has been very good, however sporadic their releases.

The 747 in Pan Am colours has been available across several scales. Here it is captured at 1/200 in the Pan Am testbed airframe with nose probe, and at 1/500 in the later large font PAN AM titles. Also seen is the early BA -100 in the very smart Landor livery, which updated an old airframe into a new era for BA.

Moulded resin/plastic models from the Wooster range were particularly popular in the 1980s and 1990s. The good quality and reasonable pricing appealed to younger and more mature enthusiasts. Larger-scale versions were later produced.

This super South African Airways (SAA) -SP from Inflight 200 at 1/200 scale really does capture the sharp lines of the shorter -SP-series 747. The unusual, earlier colour scheme of the airline really added to the look – especially the unique reverse-strake on the nose running through the flight-deck windows.

Up close the former SAA colours and the -SP's style rendered so well make this a standout collectors' item for -SP fanatics. The wing panelling is of note too.

Above: ZS-SPB and the Springbok looking great on this high-quality rendering. Note the very accurate wing-skin detailing on the tailplane. In 1997, SAA replaced the Springbok emblem and the old national colours of orange, white and blue with a new livery based upon the new national flag, with a sun motif. The airline's name on its aircraft was changed from the Afrikaans name Suid-Afrikaanse Lugdiens to South African. As a symbol of the new rainbow nation.

The Pratt & Whitney JT9D engine and casing captured in superb quality.

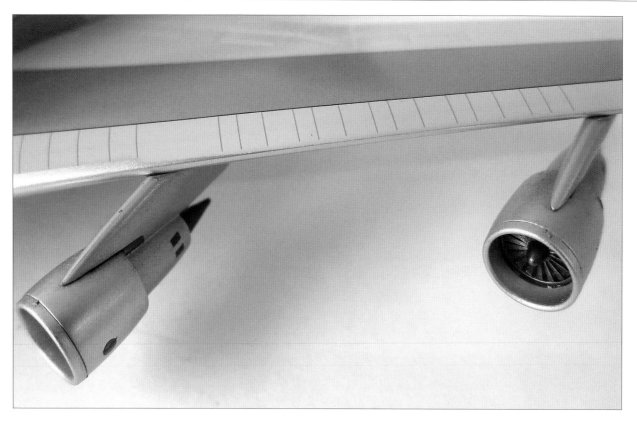

Two Pratts, pylons and panel work – the quality you expect from 1/200 and at the purchase cost requested.

The -SP served several Middle Eastern governments and special/royal flights, with the last such -SP arriving into the region as late as 1987. Here we see Inflight 200's rendition of the -SP(-21) registered VP-BAT of the Qatari Amiri Flight (ex-Pan Am, United) as used by Sheikh Khalifa Bin Hamad al Thani, in its exquisite livery which was only excelled by its amazing VIP interior configuration with state rooms and bedrooms. This model is nearly 11 inches long and has a near 12-inch wingspan and costs over $200 new.

Top: As late as 2020 this airframe remained viable at over 42 years old and was reputed to be reregistered following its sale as N7477S to CSDS LLC. Inflight 200's release of the model in 2019 in such niche colours proved that the -SP following is significant.

Above: Another view of the Inflight 200 747-SP seen with the same casting in the Qatari -SP. This -SP casting was spot on and has a huge following among -SP devotees in all the respective liveries. This early SAA livery with the nose-strake paint design is now a rare item on this model.

Left: Seen from above, the perfect scaling of the -SP is seen alongside its detailing of windows, wipers and antennae.

Pan Am's *Clipper Storm King* (1969 era) was released in flight-test trials configuration with a 32-foot nose probe attached. This is another piece of 747 history captured by Inflight 200 at 1/200 scale and really one for the serious collector. A version with the nose probe painted in high-visibility red and white was also released and is a rarity.

Even at 1/400 scale, details can be accurate. This China Clipper II displays the ultra-large-font PAN AM titling. Rarer Pan Am 747 scale models include those marked Moscow Express, a name of a Pan Am 747 over which much modelling and enthusiast argument exists. Was it actually applied to the -100 N733PA as some say? Rare models of Pan Am's named 747s now sell for big money even at smaller scale.

A Wooster model in plastic depicting the very unusual Avianca of Colombia livery – a sound basic model of a moulding that brought joy to many.

The later Cathay Pacific colours on the Sky Classics -400 model of VR-HUI – not perfect and with a couple of printing issues such as the flight-deck windows, but nevertheless a nice display model in plastic at an accessible price for the enthusiast if not the expert and forensic av geek.

Herpa excelled in small-scale diecast 747s (at 1/500 and 1/400 Herpa Wings). This Qantas -200 in the older Qantas ochre livery also featured the limited edition boxing kangaroo tailfin which was a short-term scheme on the real aircraft, so the model is rare too. A Blue Box-branded version was also marketed at 1/400. Qantas created a second boxing kangaroo livery for its -400 VH-OJU, and Herpa modelled that at 1/500 as well.

Big Bird is a brand of curious provenance but produces small birds of 1/500 scale that have excellent detailing in moulding/casting and livery printing terms. GeminiJets' small-scale 747s may rightly proliferate, but Big Bird's offering is not to be underestimated. This was the Big Bird Landor livery BA -100, and very smart it was too.

747 Scale

The earliest 747 scale-model kits included Airfix and the Revell mouldings of the early 1970s. **Airfix** were quick off the mark with their tooling up and ready for late 1969. By early 1970, Airfix had marketed its -100 at 1/144 scale in BOAC markings and were soon also to depict a Braniff Big Orange-liveried Airfix 747 which latterly expanded the range and sales appeal, not least in the UK. An Airfix-USA dedicated box version appeared. Of note, Airfix went with an early Air France 747 release featuring the classic AF livery. A series of Airfix 747s Sky Kings and Modern Airliners ranges offered differing liveries of the top 747 operators and relevant box art, but relied upon original -100/-200 depictions and toolings. Modellers began to modify the kits into their own renditions. In 1987 an **Airfix/ Lodela**-branded special edition release of the 747 at 1/144 was marketed with BA or Alitalia decal sets.

The Airfix 747 was well scaled yet the tailfin seemed rather thick and some modellers questioned the wing dihedral angle and modified it. Subsequent Airfix British Airways liveries extended to the Negus (1974–84), Landor (1984–97) and the later Chatham Dockyard (1997–2020) dated schemes. The Airfix tooling seemed to reappear under **MPC** branding in 1971, wearing American Airlines decals – a very rare kit today.

Revell had launched a 747 kit by early 1974, notably with United Airlines classic markings, as well as with Pan Am, TWA and Lufthansa transfer liveries. Revell's subsequent KLM-blue -200 has been a longstanding 747 modellers' market favourite. From 1974 to 1986 new decals were offered and in 1993 a new tooling arrived. Revell offered 747 kits across several differing scales and levels of complexity and moulding finesse and numbered ability levels.

Of interest, in 1974 Revell also produced, at 1/144 scale, an airline agents-style cutaway display model of the -200B. The original issue featured United Airlines colours on the box art, but the re-issues up to 2006 had box art that depicted the often-forgotten SAS 747 livery. Revell have of course issued an excellent -400 kit. They also produced earlier 747 variants at 1/390 and 1/450 scales.

Revell/Congost would produce a 1/144-scale -200 in Iberia colours for the 1980s. **Revell/Monogram** produced a -400 at 1/144 in 1993, depicted in the then United Airlines colours.

As early as 1984, Revell were producing a 1/144-scale 747 E-4B Command Post edition. Revell then went all out with new liveries for its -200 and -400 models to cover major airlines and special editions such as the Iron Maiden 747. By 2013, a Lufthansa -800 was offered at 1/144 scale. For the 50th anniversary of the 747, Revell produced a 1/144 model of the -100 in Boeing house livery.

Building on its success with its 1/144 scale -400, Revell created a new tooling for the -800 self-build kit at its Grade Five level. This included the more unusual -800F in the United Parcel Service specification. Although the actual mouldings seem a bit underwhelming in white plastic when taken from the box, they are well-scaled and build into a fine model – with a small amount of expert modeller work.

The well-scaled main gear seen in the deployed-for-landing setting with the main gear doors hanging down. On the full-size 747, these doors retract when the wheels are down for takeoff to reduce drag and re-open to accept the undercarriage back up into the body in a nineteen-second retraction cycle

Of note, the freighter version of the -800 used the old short-top, upper-deck lobe from the 747's original design. This Revell kit captured its contours and scaling very well.

Revell got the size and scale of the 747 fin correct and the rudder sections are also well moulded. Note the APU exhaust outlet and correct setting of the tailplane.

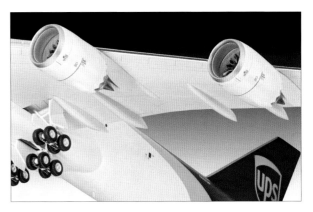

The -800's new engine pylons, special engine casings and simpler flaps-section design were well captured in this model. It is vital for the modeller to set the engines on their pylons at the correct angle.

The -800I (for Intercontinental) is likely to be Lufthansa's post-Covid flagship and must have two decades of life in it. So the superb Revell 800I in Lufthansa colours suddenly seems highly appropriate. This is a great 1/144 scale model of the post-2015 747 and really does it justice. A bit of patient work on the mouldings and detailing at the build stage can turn this into a great kit at a very reasonable price.

This is how good the front undercarriage can be made to look with the time and skills to create a high quality rendering in plastic. Some more skin detailing to the lower fuselage might improve things too.

The passenger version of the -800 uses the long-top, extended upper deck from the -400 airframe's toolings, but is longer – as is the forward fuselage. Revell got the changes spot on and again the shaping, scaling and vital aerodynamic contours are all excellent.

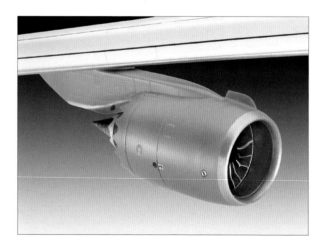

Crucial to the -800 plot are the new engines and their revised mounting pylons that are very different from the old- 400s. Also deployed were serrated-edged casings to reduce noise and improve local airflow. All these features are vital to modelling the -800 correctly.

The main gear models well if you are prepared to put the hours in. The under-body detailing and wing parts are very well modelled here. Note the finish to the engine exhaust cone.

Nitto issued a 747 kit in 1971 as a new tooling in Pan Am box art with RIKO branding. **Entex Industries** latterly produced a release of the Nitto moulding at 1/144 of the passenger 747 wearing full Flying Tigers or United livery. **Heller** produced the 747 at 1/125 and this kit was well received. **Advent** produced a derived tooling under its brand in 1979. **Trumpeter** began a range of newly tooled 747 variations from 1998 onwards at 1/144 scale.

Other key names of the 747-scale model world include **Hasegawa**, **Advent** and **Hobbycraft**. Latterly, brands such as **Hogan**, **Anigrand Craftswork**, **Witty**, and of interest the more recent **Zvezda** 1/144 model of the -800. Revell mouldings were retooled under other licences. Hasegawa created an improved tooling for the late 1990s with a 1/200 kit. As late as 2010, **Dragon** produced a 1/144 kit of the VC25A Air Force One.

Welsh Models gave modellers a new tooling of an SAA -SP in original livery in the early 2000s and went on to create variations including a TWA-marked -SP (31). Further liveries (and decal sets) covered the -SP with Pan Am and the Qantas colours. Welsh Models also produced a lovely Skyliners BOAC -136 of resin-cast and white metal parts and Welsh Models are now niche 747 items of interest.

Zvezda launched its 1/144-scale -800 in Boeing Demonstrator livery box art in 2012. The likes of GeminiJets Phoenix, Acroclassics, Dragon Wings, Schabak and Schuco have also created interesting 747 models across most of the aircraft's variants and liveries. Diecast models at varying scales have become a collectors' corner for the 747 enthusiast.

747 Modelling Notes

Depending on the tooling, age, material and variant of your chosen kit, more, or less, work may be required to create an accurate rendition of your specific 747 focus. As ever, preparation out of the box is vital. Initial work on sprues, moulding excess, flashing, dimpling and mould edges and lines can reap rewards in the finished model. Many hours of fine-tuning, cutting, sanding and honing are required on some kits, and even the best kit can benefit from such prebuild finessing.

Key issues with the basic 747 kit and its later derivatives seem to revolve around kit manufacturers' renditions of the fin, main wings, their dihedral angle, and the pylon and wingtip designs. Fuselage panel moulding and undercarriage quality are also cited across the expert modellers' forums. Expert modellers have, of course, invested huge amounts of time and labour into improving 747 kits and creating hybrids and self-built renditions.

Before focusing on liveries, paint details, weathering and in-service additions, 747 modellers have centred on creating superbly detailed airframes in grey to represent the correct structural and technical features. Adding extended flaps and slats, in-service weathering and skin repairs, and more detailed engine components are key areas of 747 model focus.

Of note, the shorter, taller 747 as the -SP variant, seems to have provided a specific vein of resin kit and diecast model enthusiasm with a huge range of liveries, technical variations and settings being chosen by dedicated modellers and diecast manufacturers.

As can be seen in the accompanying photos, the larger-scale 747 mouldings

Herpa has produced a range of smaller-scale 747s. This Air Namibia SP was one of their cheaper offerings, yet it had a naïve charm all of its own in that it made diecast accessible to the younger enthusiast.

are very accurate, yet even they require some level of preparation and modification to achieve the higher level of expertise. Mould marks, dimpling, sprue tensions and surface detailing can all be improved upon. Fuselage and other details can be reworked in the plastic, and etching technology now allows some superb effects to be added. What is vital is that the basic 747 mould captures the correct fuselage contours, wing angles, planforms and aerofoil shapes. Get these right and the 747 looks right.

As can be seen in the accompanying photographs of the moulded resin/plastic Revell offerings at two different scales, despite such differences in scale (larger models are easier to detail, mould, cast and manufacture), the modeller can soon tell if the model has been correctly researched, rendered and moulded. Older toolings will require some work on the parts prior to construction, and the modeller will of course make improvements using the range of available techniques and materials.

Revell have always excelled and a recent range of -400s, and now the -800F at 1/144 scale, really have allowed kit-builders to express their skills. Although some preparation work is required on the parts: careful modelling can produce great results. Boeing licensed Revell and Revell have got the scales and gauges correct in this plastic kit of 167 parts. Just remember to weight the nose a touch before gluing together.

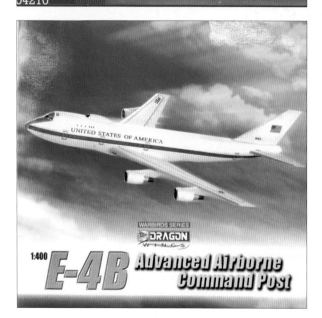

Key Details for 747 modellers

Correct fuselage detailing for variant and airline option.

Fuselage shape and scaling.

-SP rear body detailing.

Wing, tailfin and rudder moulding standards and aerofoil and chord scaling.

Wing-to-fuselage joining/dihedral and moulding.

Tailplane/horizontal stabilizer incidence setting.

Accurate upper-deck window configurations according to exact airframe.

Accurate engine types and pylon scaling and detailing.

Intake, casing, fan blade and exhaust details and design differences.

Main door and cargo door moulding standards and in-service reinforcement plates.

Realistic slat and flap details and configurations.

Antenna, strobe and other external fittings.

Windows and blanking accuracy.

Undercarriage settings and tyre mouldings and strut detailing.

Rear underbody rendition (outflow vents, skin details, dimpling, etc.).

APU details accuracy.

Correct colours, hues and livery according to date or use on specific airframe/registration chosen.

Airframe difference between passenger, mixed-Combi and freighter variants.

-400 and -800 details and differences.

Flight deck and cabin details.

Engine casings and engine blow-in vent door on early 747s, circa 1970.

Top left: The earlier Revell -200 at 1/390 scale was good but small and rather flat in its detailing. It made a nice kit for many a young modeller.

Top right: KLM again. At 1/450 scale, this kit was just big enough to reward with detail as a -200 – in any livery you liked, of course.

Above: Dragon Wings produced several 747s in several scales, but this E4-B was rare and rightly popular, especially with its airframe differences such as the lobe upon upper-deck lobe capturing the E4-B's essence.

747 Detailing

Today, a wide range of kits, decals, detailing, etching and technical modification accessories mean that the modeller can create very accurate 747 renditions and also build specials and rare examples of actual airframes. Differing engines, their respective alternative pylons, wing roots, winglets, flaps, cargo doors, upper-deck variations and military airframe variations are all catered for by specialist model-747 accessory providers, such as **26 Decals**, **Scale Model Parts**, **Bra Z Models**, **Hogan**, **Transport Wings**, **Scale Aircraft Conversions** and **Welsh Models**. A range of great livery decals is available from the likes of 26 Decals, Bra Z, as well as **Flightpath**, **KV Models** and **Airwaves**.

Painting/spraying the fuselage and aircraft skin has also become a modeller's art form and perfect preparation can yield stunning results. Ensuring the correct skin panel detailing is a key area of 747 model focus. Referral to airframe photographs can allow the modeller to add the in-service reinforcements, maintenance and airworthiness directive applications to the 747 across its 50 years of operation.

The expert modeller can focus on matching differing engine types and even such types' own variations via bought-in or hand-made modification parts. What of later-series Pratt & Whitney or Rolls-Royce RB11-524 D- or G/H-series, or later GE engines? The mouldings and parts are all out there, as they are for Air Force One or USAF 747 E4B variants.

The modeller can therefore render anything from an early Avianca 747 livery, or a rare Pan Am scheme, to military schemes, or numerous 1970s–1980s airline markings from such suppliers' ranges.

Livery or colour scheme design for the 747 is a major area where the actual aircraft and the scale-model aircraft offer over hundreds of options. Major airlines and lesser-known airlines all created probably the most expensive and complex set of airframe liveries ever created and the modeller can now take advantage of modern decal and printing technology to create the livery of their choice.

Stands, display in-flight positions, flap settings, undercarriage up or down, cabin doors open at static display – all these themes can now be applied to the modelling of the 747 across its diverse type variations, operator liveries and eras. Perhaps now, more than ever before, the scale-model enthusiast can create a tribute to probably the most influential airline transport achievement in the history of man's flight.

This Revell -400 model was constructed by James Argaet to top-level skills in the stunning SAA livery of the modern era. Livery kits on the decal market make models like this easily possible. Extra detailing went into the finish, notably on wings, skins and engine details, demonstrating just what many hours of painstaking modelling can achieve.

Tower Air were a well-known second-tier American 747 operator with a loyal following who scooped up ex-premier carrier airframes.

Speedbird heading home. British Airways 747-436 captured in a painting by the author as seen on finals to London Heathrow Airport under a typical Heathrow sky.

Acknowledgements

With thanks to Aviation Retail Direct and Paul Burge, the late Jon Proctor, *Airliners* magazine, *Airways* magazine, *Diecast Flyer*, *Model Airliner*, *Unofficial Airfix Forum*, Boeing Commercial Aircraft Press Office and photo archive, British Airways Press Office, Cathay Pacific Press Office, Lufthansa Press Office, KLM Press Office, Qantas (London) and Qantas (Sydney) and its Jetbase staff, 26 Decals, Cotswold Airport, Heathrow Airport Ltd, Flughafen Frankfurt Main, Amsterdam Schiphol Airport and Air Salvage International Ltd.

Photographs: principal photographs are by Lance Cole and other sources as indicated, including Boeing, BA, Lufthansa, Qantas and Aviation Retail Direct. Reference sources include the author at Airlife Publishing via *Long Haul, Heavies*, and other works including *Boeing 747 Classic* by P. Gilchrist, Airlife Publishing Ltd; also, *747: Creating the World's First Jumbo Jet and Other Adventures from a Life in Aviation* by J. Sutter and J. Spenser; Boeing's 747 press materials 1968 to date; communications with Boeing; Sam Chui public content; *Flight International* archive; and NASM Washington D.C.. Please note the author, Lance F. Cole, has no connection to any website, works and/or photography service citing 'Lance Cole Photography'.